Raspberry Pi

The Complete Beginner's Guide To Raspberry Pi 3: Learn Raspberry Pi In A Day - A Comprehensive Introduction To The Basics Of Raspberry Pi & Computer Programming

Steve Gold

Table of Contents

Introduction

What is a Raspberry Pi?

The Raspberry Pi is a wonderful small, inexpensive device that can be plugged into a screen, and can be controlled with a normal keyboard and mouse. It is extremely versatile and allows one to explore many facets of modern technology. It is able to connect to the Internet, act a first class media center, as well as execute computer tasks like spreadsheet creation, word processing, and games. For the more technically minded it also allows programming in a variety of computer languages.

In addition to the above, much work is being done with Raspberry Pi to interact with what is called the *Internet of Things,* which means with the physical world, and it has been used in a wide array of such applications. This book will guide you in your first steps in this very important field.

Why Raspberry Pi?

Why so much trouble to develop a device for tasks done very well with computers, tablets, and even phones? Raspberry Pi was designed with the aim of enhancing learning, thought, and experimenting, particularly in the young. The Pi is a very powerful, little device, but costs no more than many textbooks.

With society ever more dependent on computers and computer technology, it is essential that people be exposed to them as much as possible.

What is a Raspberry Pi 3 ?

The Raspberry Pi 3 is the latest version and is very similar to its predecessors. However, it is much quicker and has built-in antennae for Bluetooth and Lan.

Chapter 1

Getting a Raspberry Pi 3

What to buy?

On going to Google or any other search engine and typing in "Raspberry Pi 3" you will get millions of hits. If you follow Raspberry Pi with the name of your state or country, such as "Raspberry Pi France" you will get thousands, possibly millions of hits. When I put "Raspberry Pi France" into Google I got a massive 529, 000 hits. The Raspberry Pi 3 is on many people's minds!

Many of the hits will refer to merchants selling the Raspberry Pi. When you find one and go to their site you will find that many different things associated with the Raspberry Pi will be on sale. If you are a complete novice then look for the *Raspberry Pi 3 Complete Starter Kit*, or something similar. I got a kit called *Raspberry Pi 3 Complete Noobs Combo.*

You might be tempted to purchase the *Raspberry Pi 3 Model B*. While this is a cheaper purchase you will still have to purchase the following in addition to the Pi: an SD card on which to put the operating system, a monitor or screen, a keyboard, a mouse, a heat sink, a power supply, an HDMI cable for connecting to a screen.

Even with a complete starter kit you will still need a monitor or screen, a keyboard, a mouse and possibly an HDMI cable to connect your screen and RPI3 (*Raspberry Pi 3 Model B*).

In the package I purchased there was:

1. An 8 GB NOOBS (new out of box software) MICRO STD CARD and ADAPTER
2. A clear case with GPIO slot
3. A 5.1V 2.5A power supply
4. Three heat sinks.

These are not included if you just purchased an RPI3 Model B.

If you insist on only getting the RPI3 Model B then you will have to load the NOOBS yourself (we'll get to what this is later) onto a MICRO STD CARD. There are many references for this with the best and simplest I have found to be https://www.youtube.com/watch?v=y4GOG4P-4tY

1. A case is useful to protect dust and other pollutants from settling on your RPI3, but certainly not essential.

2. You may opt for a power supply, which you might have at home rather than get one specifically for the RPI3. If you do this you must ensure that the one you're using is compatible with the RPI3. Most power supplies at home are cell phone chargers, and there are great differences among

them. You may find that the power supply using a cell phone charger is adequate however remember that the purpose of such a charger is to charge cell phones and not the RPI3. The cost of a power supply for an RPI3 is quite low and a complete beginner is strongly advised to get one. The electrical requirements of an RPI3 are 5.1 V DC and 2.5A. If your different source supply cannot supply this then do not be surprised if it is inadequate.

3. Heat sinks are a precaution to prevent your RPI3 from overheating. Normal use of an RPI3, particularly without a case, should not lead to overheating. The uses outlined in this book should not lead to overheating. Despite that if you are provided with heat sinks then it will no harm to

attach them as instructed. Doing so is recommended.

4. Another thing, which you should consider that is not included in many starter kits, is a USB Micro inline switch. The use of these on any RPI3 is recommended in order to power it down. Without one it is necessary to either use the GUI, which would be simplest for most users, or, for the more technically minded, a command line method. Pulling out the plug from the power input is not suitable for powering down. Doing this could seriously damage the STD card. A USB Micro inline switch provides a safe way of switching off your RPI3, much akin to switching the lights off. It is probably not necessary to get one immediately, but it is a very sensible addition eventually.

In order to begin to apply the RPI3 physically, a *breadboard* is necessary. This is a board, which enables experimentation with circuits without having to do any soldering. Many suitable breadboards are available however there is a breadboard made specifically for the RPI3 called the RPI- BBOARD. There is no need to get one initially but as soon as the user of an RPI3 starts to create circuits a suitable breadboard will be essential.

Other purchases can be made as the need arises. Applications of the RPI3 to the *Internet of Things* may need sensors such as card readers, thermometers, touch-screens, humidity meters, barometers, motion detectors and gas detectors. In addition, you may wish to use a camera. Most RP3 dealers have a wide variety of add-ons however it is certainly not necessary to get them initially.

Chapter 2

Components and Terminology of Computers

Raspberry Pi?

What is it about the Raspberry Pi that justifies the expense of getting one? As was mentioned in the introduction, it was designed with the aim of enhancing learning, thought, and experimenting, particularly in the young. All of these laudable aims can be achieved very well with an ordinary laptop or computer so why to bother with a Raspberry Pi? The diagram below offers one reason. No other functioning device shows, so clearly, the different components of a computer. This chapter runs over these, as it is very difficult to really get a grasp on this technology, which plays such an important role in modern life, and is destined to be even more important in the future without such knowledge.

Hardware and Software

These are two terms we will frequently use. Most readers are probably familiar with them, however in case you're not.

Computer hardware is the physical part of a computing system. Included are the case, monitor, keyboard, mouse hard drive, motherboard, USB sticks, and more.

Computer software is the collection of programs that the computer runs. This includes the operating system, which consists of inbuilt programs to perform all the functions the computer executes, as well as all the other programs such as word processors, web browsers, programming languages, games and so much more. On the Raspberry Pi, these are all stored on the Micro SD card, which is so important.

Diagram of the Raspberry Pi 3

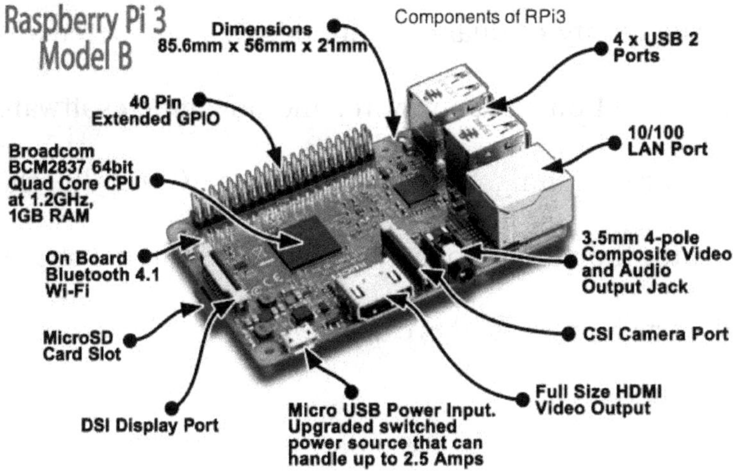

Most computers have:

CPU

The CPU is that part of the computer where the vast majority of executions take place. CPUs have cores. A single core is a single processing unit that executes calculations. Dual core means a CPU which two calculation units or two processing units. The contrast in the ability of dual core and single core systems is dependent on what software, and how much software you are running on your machine. Generally the greater the number of cores the better. The Raspberry Pi 3 has four cores. It is capable of a lot.

Case

The case is the container for most of the hardware of a computer. It is necessary for this to be a safe, secure place. In most desktop computers it is easily recognized as a box with wires coming into it. In laptops (notebooks) the case is a plastic covering. In some computers such as the newer Apples the case is the screen. The Raspberry Pi is almost unique in that it does not have a case. When you get you see it is tiny in comparison to other computers. There are cases available. It is up to you as to whether you get one.

Power supply

This is the electricity used to make the computer work. Mains power is AC (alternating current) and is too strong for most computers. Computers have a piece of machinery, which receives the AC and turns it into the DC (direct current) of much lower strength for the computer. Laptops have this. They also have a battery, which can provide power. Batteries need recharging and often, particularly with older laptops the battery has a very short life. Many users of laptops use the mains as the primary power source.

The Raspberry Pi only needs a very small amount of power 5 V 2.5A. You may find that the power supply using a cell phone charger is adequate, however, remember that the purpose of such a charger is to charge cell phones and not the RPI3. The cost of a power supply for an RPI3 is quite low; a complete beginner is strongly advised to get one.

RAM

RAM (random access memory) is the place in a computer where the operating system, application programs, and data in current use are kept so that they can be quickly reached by the computer's processor. RAM is much faster to read from and write to than the other kinds of storage in a computer, the hard disk, a USB, or a DVD. However, the data in RAM stays there only as long as your computer is running. When you turn the computer off, RAM loses its data. When you turn your computer on again, your operating system and other files are once again loaded into RAM, usually from your hard disk. The Raspberry Pi 3 has 1GB of RAM.

Motherboard

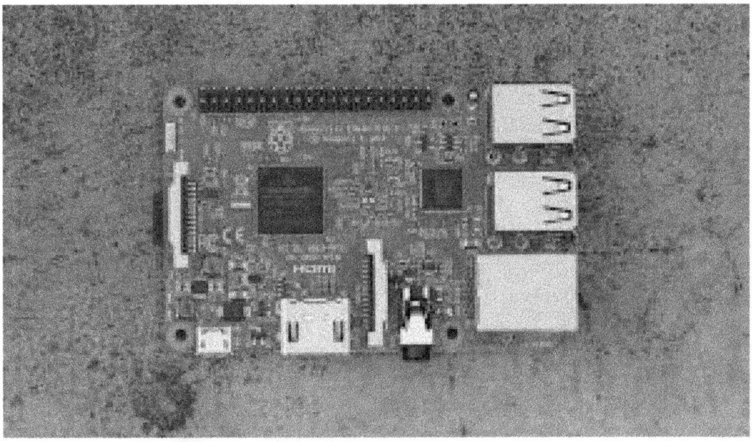

The motherboard is the main printed circuit board (PCB) in computers . It contains most crucial electronic components of the system, such as the central processing unit(CPU) and memory, and provides connections for what are called peripherals. The motherboard in a Raspberry Pi 3 is the green item you hold when you pick one up.

BUS

The BUS is the circuitry which connects components in computers . It varies from computer to computer. The bus in a Raspberry Pi 3 is only readily visible under a magnifying glass. It is seen as the faint lines connecting the different components.

On-board components (eg video, USB ports, and networking)

On-board describes a piece of hardware that is found on a circuit board. Unlike hardware, such as sticks and cards, these components should not be removed from their computer; however, they can be disabled through software, if necessary. Obvious examples in the case of the Raspberry Pi 3 are the Camera Serial Interface for connecting to a camera, the Display Serial Interface for connecting to a touch screen, the GPIO for electronics, the Audio Output Jack, the Bluetooth, and Wi-Fi.

Storage

Most storage of data in laptops is on the hard drive(s), which can be magnetic, optical, or solid state drive(s). It is not the intention of this chapter to give a precise definition of these. Suffice to say that they exist, and the storage of the Raspberry Pi 3 is on the Micro SD card which you will purchase, either with the required software on it or that you can put on it, using the download from https://www.raspberrypi.org/downloads/ .

Peripherals

A peripheral device is any extra device that connects to and works with the computer. Some well-known peripherals are listed below and how they apply to the Raspberry Pi. Although most of you will know what each of the following peripherals is, I've included a brief description for the complete beginners.

Keyboard

A computer keyboard is probably the best-known peripheral. It is an input device that allows a person to enter symbols like letters and numbers into a computer. Although there are many kinds of the keyboard the type most people expect is the QWERTY design, based on typewriter keyboards. The Raspberry Pi does not come with a keyboard. It is necessary to obtain your own.

Mouse

A computer mouse is a well-known input device, commonly used with personal computers. Moving a mouse along a flat surface moves the on-screen cursor to different positions on the screen. Items can be moved or selected by pressing the mouse buttons (often called clicking). The Raspberry Pi does not come with a mouse. It is necessary to obtain your own.

CRT Monitor

CRT is the abbreviation for Cathode-Ray Tube. In this now obsolete technology electron beams within a monitor move across a screen interacting with phosphor dots on the inside glass tube. Obviously, the Raspberry Pi does not come with one, however, if you have one, and you are an advanced user, then it would be an interesting project to achieve a successful interaction.

LCD Monitor

This is a flat panel screen, which uses the liquid crystal display and is connected to a computer. Laptops have always used LCD screens, and now LCD monitors are the main method of display for desktops.

Prior to about 2004, the large CRT monitors were the main method of display for desktops.

It is possible to connect a Raspberry Pi to a laptop although it involves some extra work. Some desktop screens cannot be fitted to the Raspberry Pi as they lack an HDMI connection. Make sure that any monitor or screen you get has an HDMI connection

Printer

You almost certainly know that a printer is a machine that takes text and graphic output from a computer and transfers it to paper or other material. There are all sorts of technologies such as dot-matrix, ink-jet, LCD, led and laser used in printers. If you own a PC or Mac you are probably used to just inserting your printer and using plug and play to fire it up. Unfortunately, such simplicity is not available with the Raspberry Pi and the process is quite involved. It will be discussed later.

Chapter 3

First Steps in Using a Raspberry Pi 3

Before you begin you must have:

1. A Raspberry Pi 3
2. A keyboard and a mouse
3. A computer screen, or a TV screen
4. A cable which has an HDMI outlet to join the screen to the Raspberry Pi 3. (v) a Micro STD card with NOOBS on it, either on it from your dealer or

downloaded from https://www.raspberrypi.org/downloads/noobs/.

5. A power source for your Raspberry Pi 3. It should be 5.1 V 2.5 A.

Once assembled:

1. You must insert the mouse cable, and the keyboard cable into USB ports on the Raspberry Pi 3;
2. Join the Raspberry Pi 3 to the monitor;
3. Connect the power source to the Raspberry Pi 3 but **do not** connect it to the mains power yet;

4. Connect the monitor to the mains and switch it on. You should see the screen with some indication that there is no signal.

The next thing you must do is to plug the power source for the Raspberry Pi 3 into the mains. As soon as you do the no signal sign will disappear from the screen to be replaced by some indication that something is happening. When you do so you will see a change, something as in the diagram below.

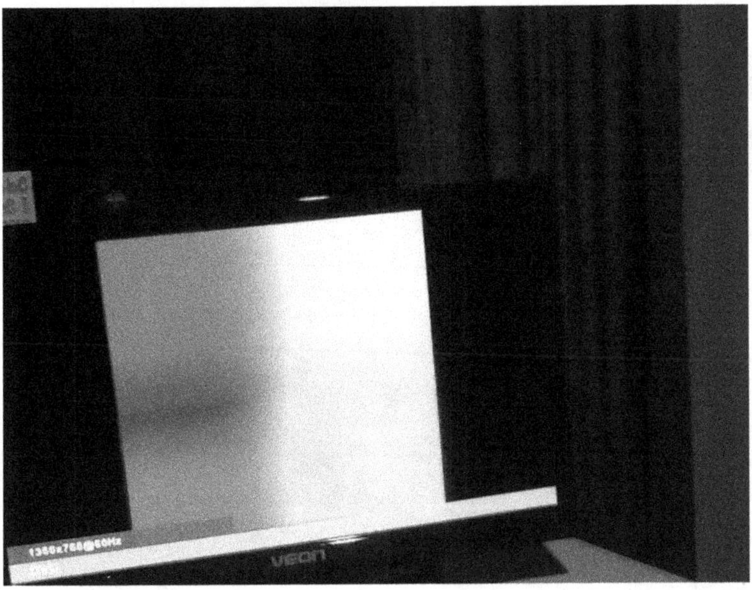

A screen of scrolling writing will follow.

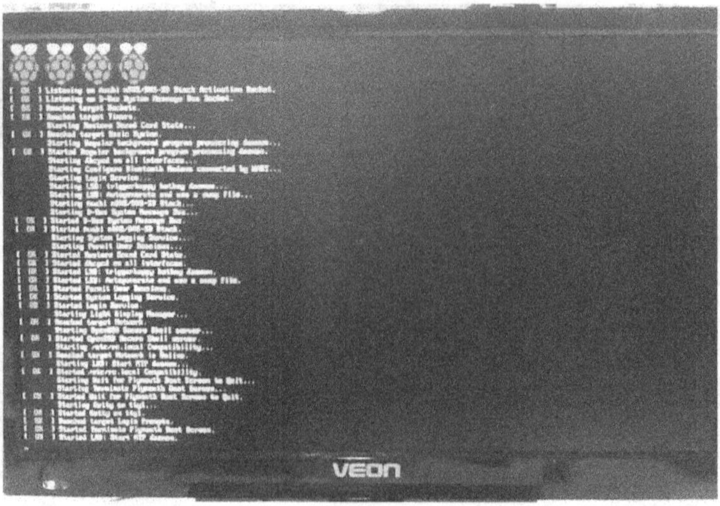

When this is finished there should be a screen with a menu of icons, most of which will not be enabled.

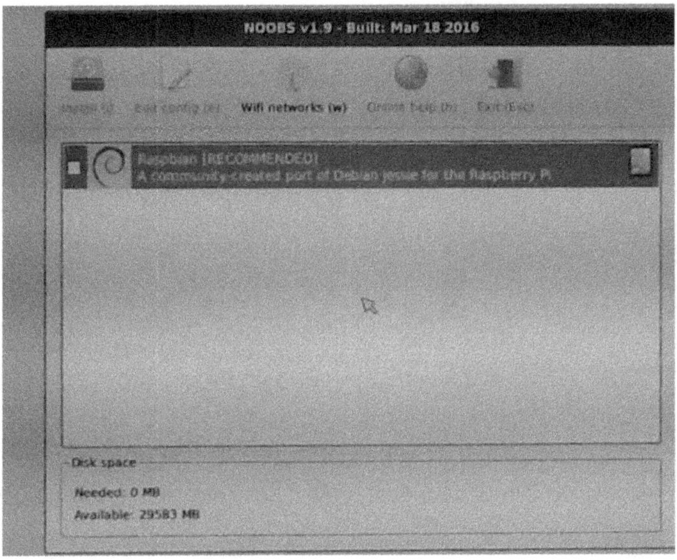

There are a number of icons along the top. Two are enabled, **Install**, and **WiFi networks(w)**. You should click this latter with your cursor. If you do the screen will change too .

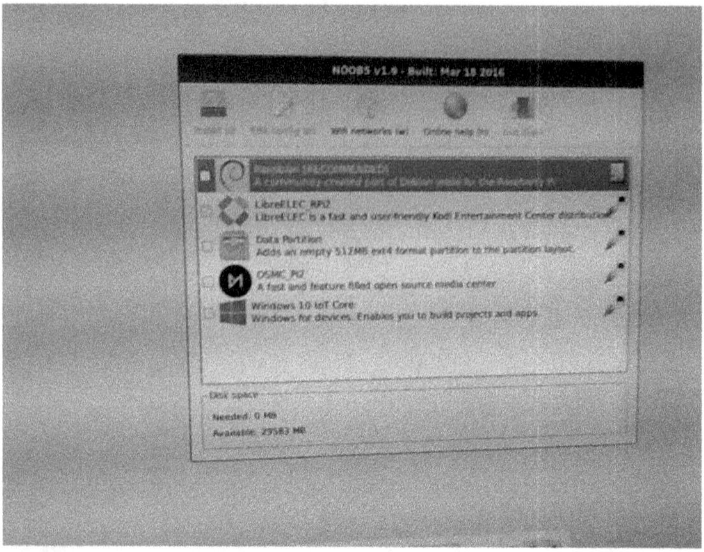

You can select as many of these as you wish then click **Install.**

You will get the following warning.

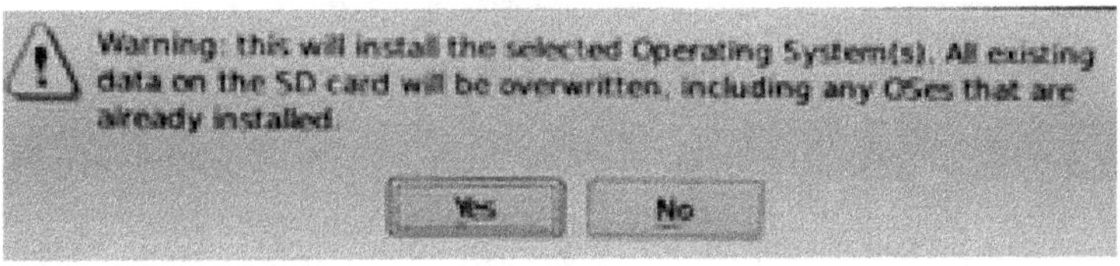

You should ignore this warning and click yes. Installation may take some time depending on your computer's specifications. While this is taking place a sequence of windows will appear. Among these is a welcome to the Raspberry Pi

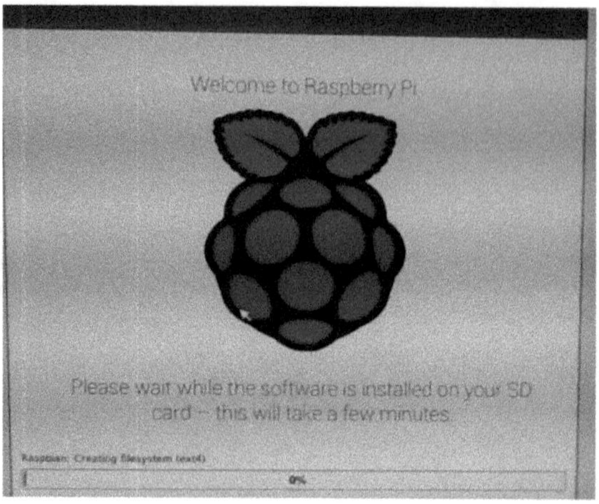

Next a number of windows, with information about some of the programs in Raspian and other programs that are being installed. The process of installation can take as long as twenty to forty minutes, again, depending on your computer's specifications. When installation is complete a window will appear indicating that the Raspian operating system has been successfully installed.

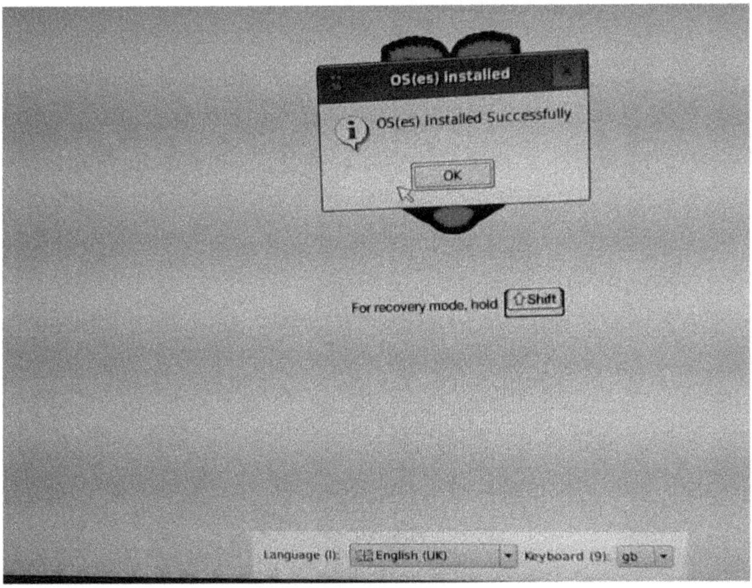

Click OK to complete. Once done the main Raspian desktop appears, as in the diagram below.

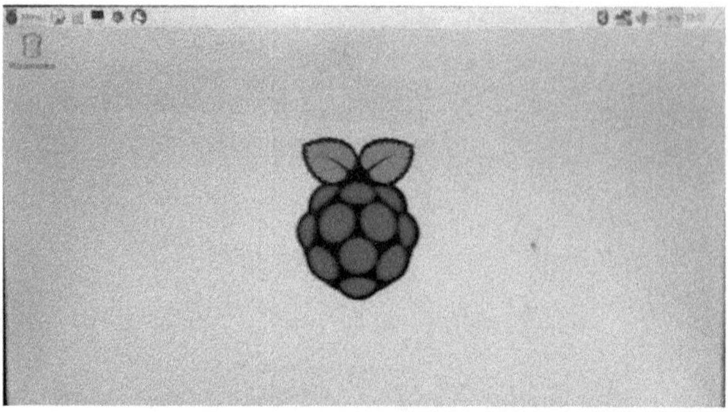

The top left part of the menu will be our next concern. This is shown more clearly in the diagram, which follows.

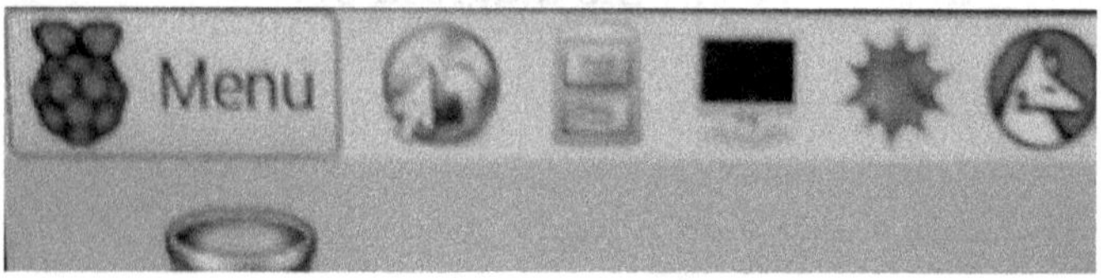

Click on the Menu button and you should get the drop down menu shown in the diagram following.

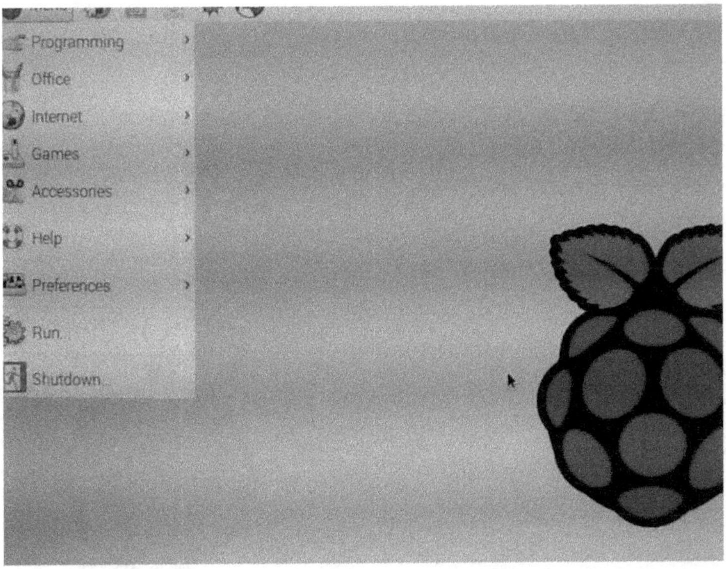

You will see a drop-down list of submenus. The submenus cover Programming, Office, Internet, Games, Accessories, Help, Preferences, Run, and Shutdown.

If you now click on the Programming submenu you

will see a number of choices:

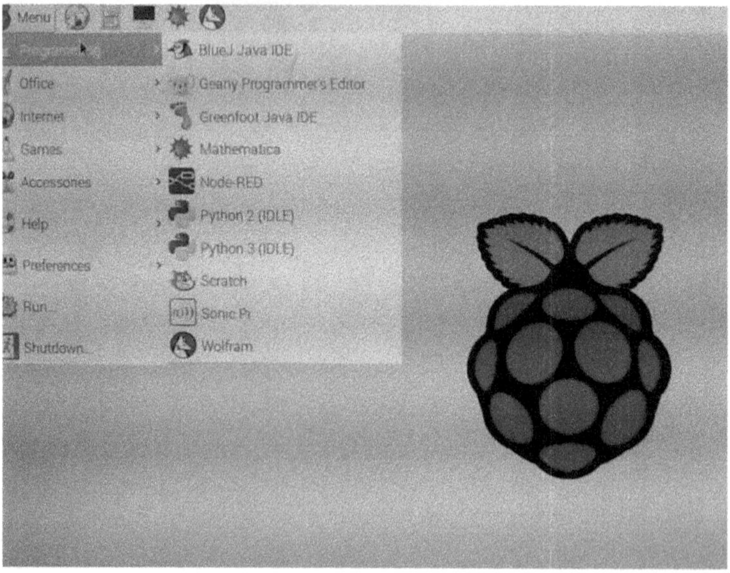

The first is the BlueJ Java IDE, the second is the Geary Programmer's Editor , etc.

The next submenu is the Office submenu. If you click on this you will notice that all of the items are in the suite of programs called LibreOffice.

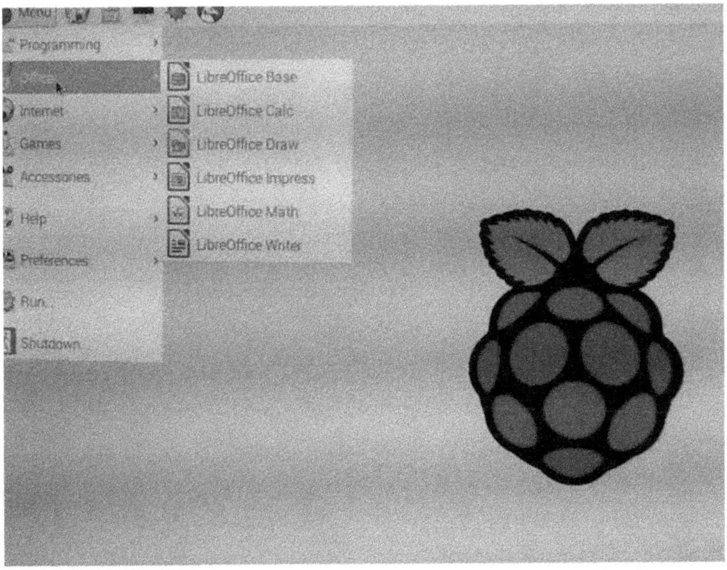

There is a database called Base, a spreadsheet called Calc, a drawing program called Draw, a presentation program, similar to PowerPoint, called Impress, a math program and finally a word processing program called Write.

The next sub-menu involves Connection to the Internet.

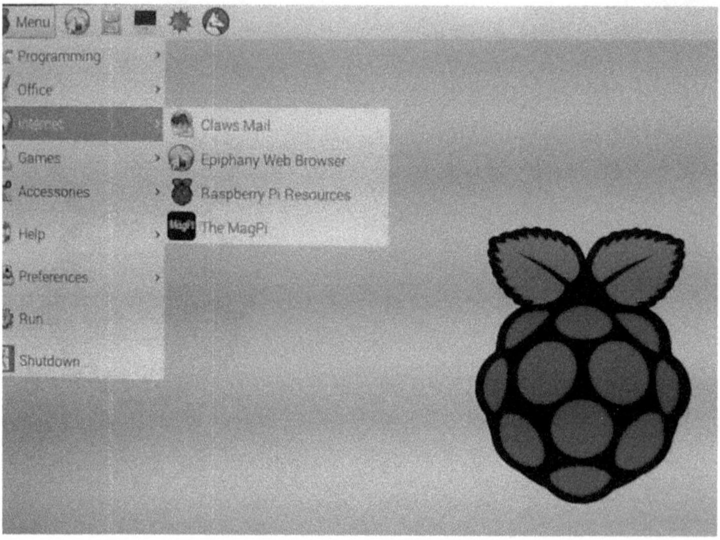

If the submenu for the Internet is clicked you will find an email client called Claws, a web browser called Epiphany (which is quite similar to Safari, Firefox, and Chrome). There are also some resources and an application called The Magpi.

The fourth sub-menu is Games.

The games available are Minecraft Pi and a number of Python games, which are called Python because they were created with the Python programming language.

Following the Games submenu is the Accessories

submenu.

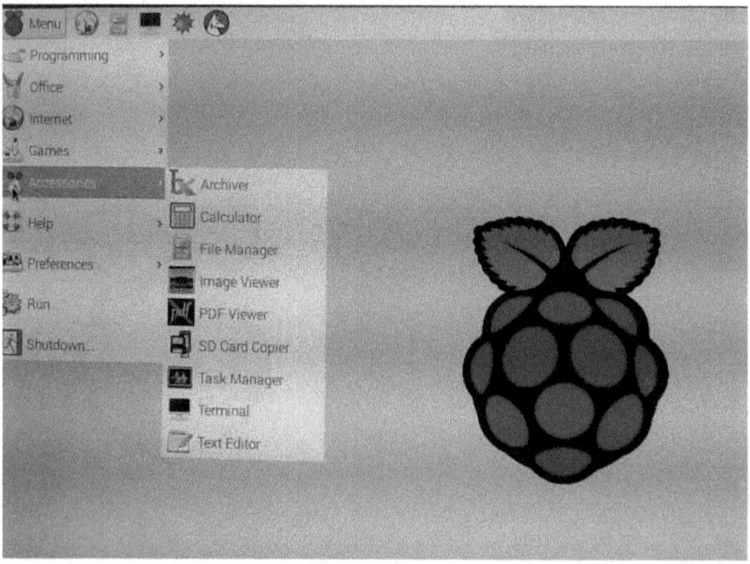

There are nine accessories, included among them, a text editor, a PDF viewer, an image viewer, a calculator, and, most important of all, a Terminal. The Help sub-menu is not shown. If you are in difficulty you may well find the answer to the problem there.

The final proper sub-menu is Preferences.

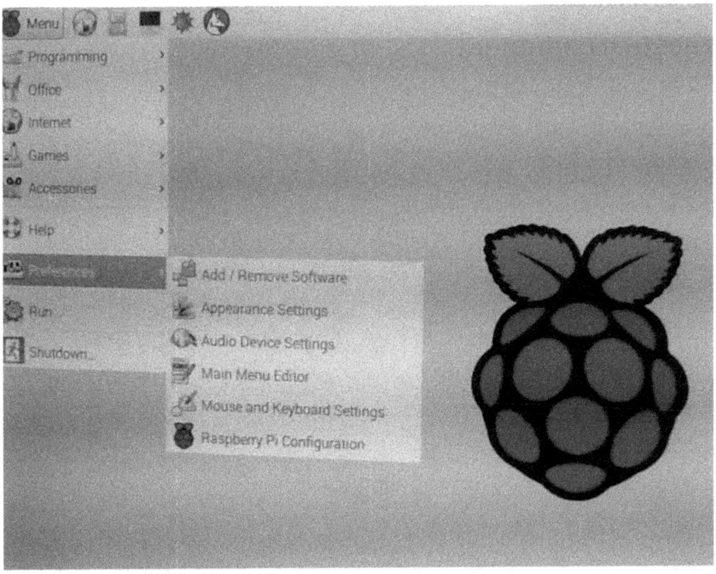

There are six preferences in this particular sub-menu. It is quite similar to the system application, which is found in both Windows and Mac operating systems.

The final two items on the menu Run and Shutdown if

you click on either of them you will not get a submenu but instead you will get a little window. The Run item when clicked gives a window with the opportunity to execute a command.

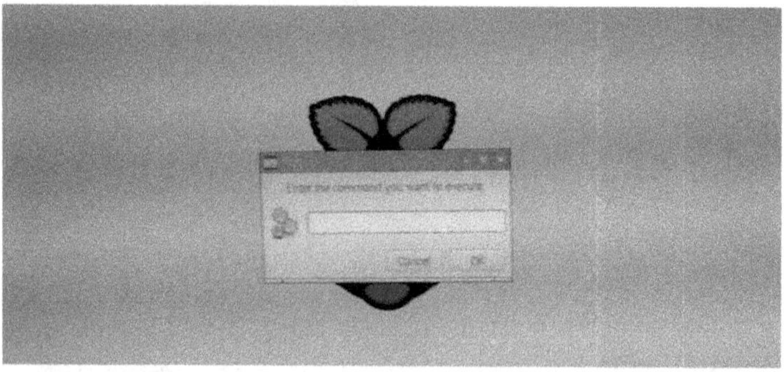

Shutdown is very important. It gives three choices, Shutdown, Reboot, and Logout.

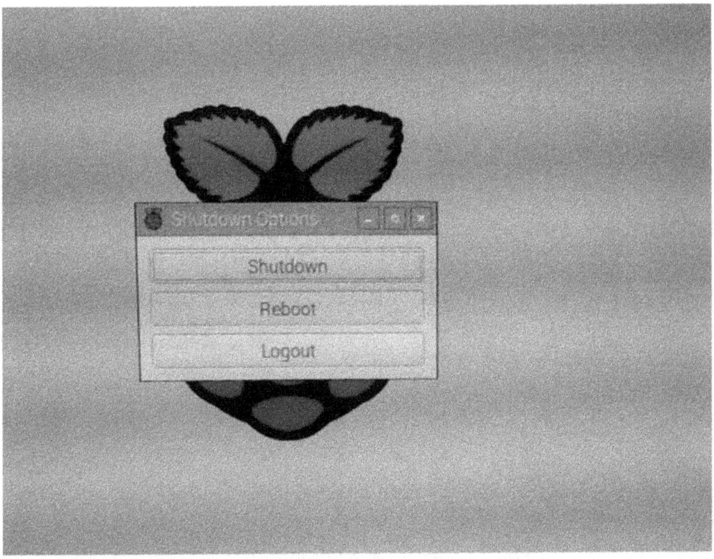

If you wish to stop your Raspberry Pi 3 it is very important that you either use this shutdown or one from the terminal. If you do not do this, and just unplug your power supply you have a very good chance of corrupting your micro disk. Don't be too frightened of doing this, as it is quite easy to format the disk then download NOOBS from https://www.raspberrypi.org/downloads/noobs/ and reinstall as described earlier.

If you click reboot you will get the window offering the different Operating Systems.

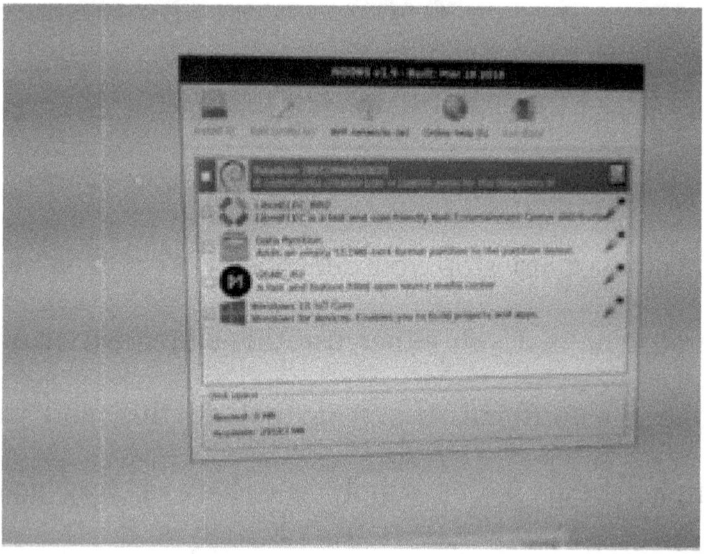

You only have a few seconds until the Operating System you were using starts again.

Chapter 4

Using the Terminal of a Raspberry Pi 3

What is the Terminal?

The Terminal is a window in which you can enter commands using a language called *Bash*. Clicking on the fourth top right icon in the menu most easily accesses this window.

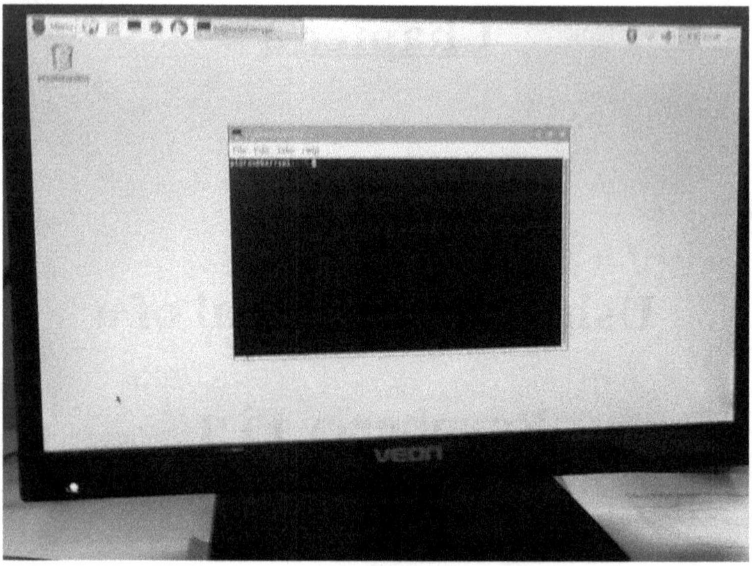

Bash scripting is easy to learn and is similar to Batch scripting in Windows using MS-DOS. Bash is very powerful. Using this approach to computing is called *Using the Command Line Interface* or *CLI* for short. This is the method by which all work on the computer used to be done. Most people have a great dislike for it, as hey find it difficult, however, with a little practice it isn't really. It takes a bit of effort but so long as you have a good reference such as http://www.circuitbasics.com/useful-raspberry-pi-commands/ , then you can copy and paste until you feel confident.

Writing then running a Shell Script on the Raspberry Pi

A shell script is nothing more than a text file consisting of a series of shell (command line) commands that are executed by the BASH shell. The shell reads the file and carries out the commands one after another. This is very convenient if it is necessary to run a large number of commands to carry out some task. Shell scripts give you the ability to automate most things using the CLI.

For those familiar with the levels of computer languages it may surprise to learn that shell languages are quite a high level programming languages. They are further from system and memory processes than lower level languages. Shell languages have commands to perform tasks using a lot of code to carry out in languages such as C, assembly language or lowest of all Machine Code.

What is possible with a shell script?

Shell scripts are particularly useful in situations requiring the entry of long sequences of commands into the command line. A majority of important computer operations can be executed with a single command if you can write a shell script for it. Some of the operations which are possible:

- Finding, creating, changing folders or files
- Creating executable files
- Updating and upgrading folders and files
- Work in batches of folders and files

- Get all sorts of information such as date, time etc.

How to create and run a shell script

In the following simple examples, we will find the working directory or folder, list its contents, create a folder, change the working folder to be the one just created,create a text file within it, display that file, then create an executable file and run it.

(1) Click on the Terminal icon to obtain the terminal window.

Then type in the following lines making sure you press enter after each one.

pwd

This is the first line of bash. It is finding out what directory (folder we are in). According to this command, we are in/home/pi

ls

This lists all the folders and files in this folder.

mkdir Exp

This creates a directory or folder called Exp

ls

List again to show Exp is there. It is.

cd /home/pi/Exp

Change directory so that we are in the directory that we just created. Notice how we have Exp behind the $. This shows we have achieved our aim of making Exp the working directory.

touch cat.txt

Creates an empty text file inside Exp called cat.txt

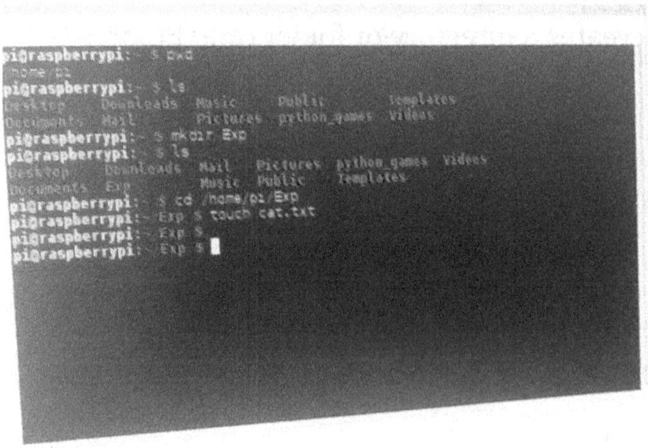

The diagram above shows how these commands and their effects appear in the terminal

nano cat.txt

This command opens cat.txt in the nano text editor. We do this to put something in this file because when it is created it is an empty file. All that is typed is the alphabet. When we have finished we press ctrl X to leave the screen. We are prompted as to whether we want to save the changes. Since we do we enter y then press Enter. This brings us back to the Terminal.

cat cat.txt

This command displays the contents of the file which is just

'abcdefghij.......yz'

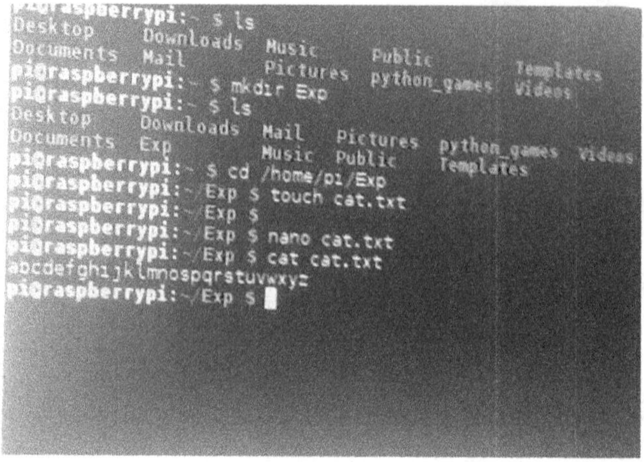
pi@raspberrypi:~ $ ls
Desktop Downloads Music Public Templates
Documents Mail Pictures python_games Videos
pi@raspberrypi:~ $ mkdir Exp
pi@raspberrypi:~ $ ls
Desktop Downloads Mail Pictures python_games Videos
Documents Exp Music Public Templates
pi@raspberrypi:~ $ cd /home/pi/Exp
pi@raspberrypi:~/Exp $ touch cat.txt
pi@raspberrypi:~/Exp $
pi@raspberrypi:~/Exp $ nano cat.txt
pi@raspberrypi:~/Exp $ cat cat.txt
abcdefghijklmnospqrstuvwxyz
pi@raspberrypi:~/Exp $

rm cat.txt

This deletes the text file cat.txt.

cd /home/pi

Change the folder back to /home/pi

rm -Rfi Exp

This deletes the folder Exp.

Having gone through some really basic commands let's create a shell script. This is going to be a very simple one.

Stay in the home folder /home/pi

Let us call the file script1.

Create an empty file script1 by

touch script1.sh

----

nano script1.sh

This opens the nano text editor.

Type the lines

#!/bin/sh

echo "The rain in Spain"

echo "Stays in the plain."

————————————————————————

The first line of this program, #!/bin/sh, is called a *shebang*. This directs the BASH shell to execute the commands in the script.

On finishing:

Exit and save the file in nano by pressing Ctrl X as we showed you before.

Now to make the script1.sh file executable. Type

sudo chmod +x script1.sh

The shell script is executable and can be run. Navigate to the directory where the file is saved, and enter either sh hello-world.sh or ./hello-world.sh.

sh script1.sh

All you get is some printed output. The script isn't very useful, however, it illustrates some basics of creating and running the shell script. Like anything else practice maketh perfect, and if you do as much scripting as possible then it will be of enormous value in your exploration of the exciting world of the Raspberry Pi 3.

Before finishing this chapter do this. Open your terminal and type in then enter

sudo -i

This means that you will be running at the correct level. Now type then enter

apt-get update;apt-get upgrade

As a result of doing this, you should get a lot of activity in your terminal. Whenever you get a prompt enter y.

Now type then enter

apt-get install iceweasel —no-install-recommends

You will a huge amount of activity in the terminal. Keep answering y, if prompted. When finished go to the *Menu* and click on *Run*.

You will get this little window.

Enter either *iceweasel* or *firefox* then press Enter or click OK.

Initially, there is nothing but after a short a window will appear asking for information. When you have finished you will have the brilliant browser *Firefox*.

Chapter 5

Connecting to the Internet Using a Raspberry Pi 3

The applications, which will be considered in this chapter, are part of the Raspian Operating System. Connection to the Internet is obviously important and this chapter will be devoted to this topic.

How do we achieve connection to the Internet?

The diagram below shows the Raspian desktop.

The left-hand menu, below, has been considered in chapter 2.

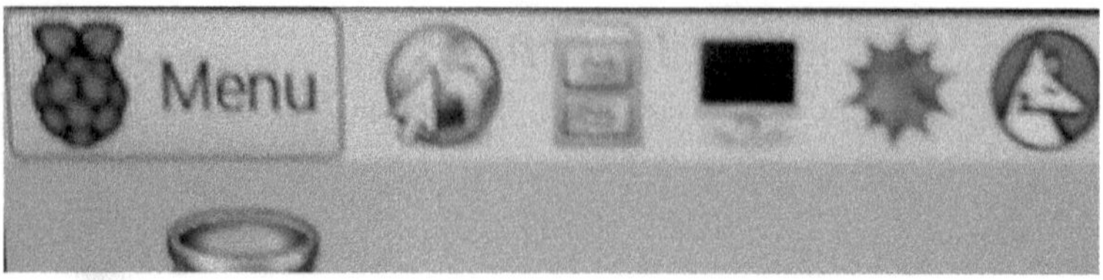

The right-hand menu will now be considered. It appears in the diagram below.

As with any menu item, you can get detailed information by 'right clicking' on that item. In the diagram below the rectangle showing a percentage has been right clicked. This percentage is CPU usage, clearly, not much is being used!

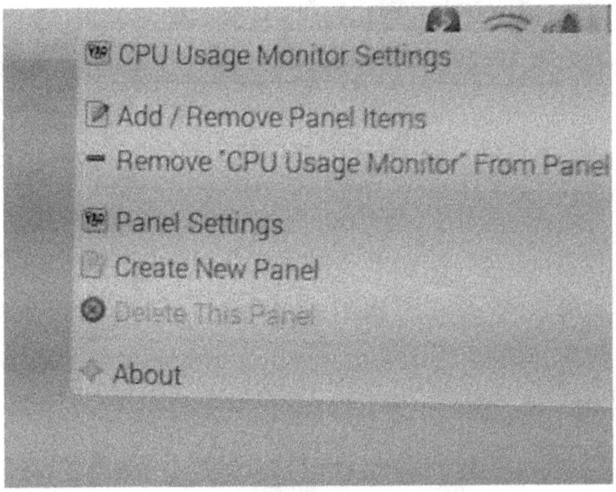

Go to the Internet menu and click on the Epiphany browser. If you have forgotten how this appears to have a look at the diagram below.

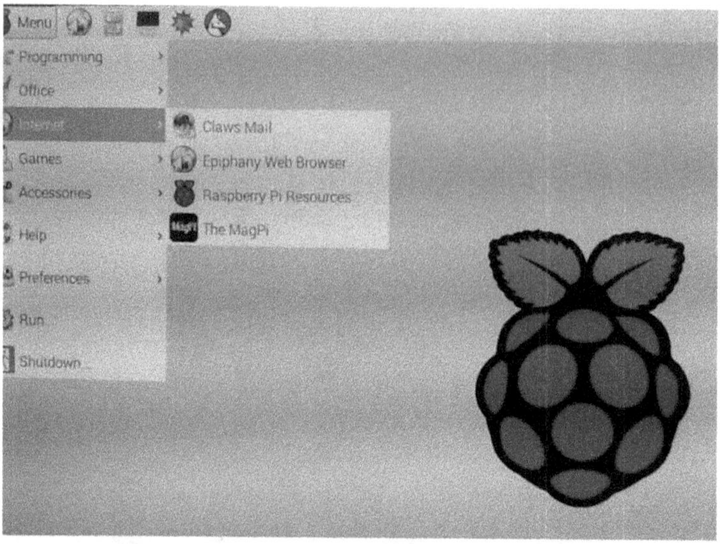

After clicking on Epiphany, you will get the window below.

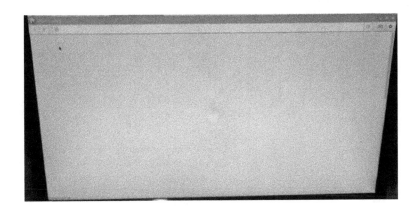

Now put www.google.com into the address bar and press Enter. If this results in the error window below, you need to put what is called a Pre-Shared Key (PSK) into the drop-down obtained by clicking on the Internet button.

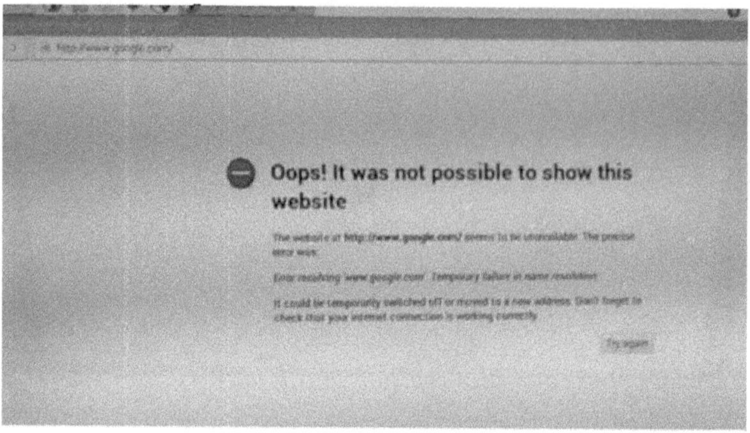

This Pre-Shared Key can be found on the back of your router.

One key feature of the browser is that it also supports MathML. This is quite significant because at the time of writing such well-known browsers as Chrome, Opera, and IE do not.

The Epiphany browser has most of the features of other better-known browsers such as Chrome, Firefox, and Safari. For most people, it will be be more than adequate.

Email

A program by which email is sent is called an email client. The Raspian Operating System provides an email client called Claws. The process of installing the Claws email client is quite straightforward. If you click on the email part of the Internet submenu you get the following window.

Click forward and you will get a window where you have to fill in personal information.

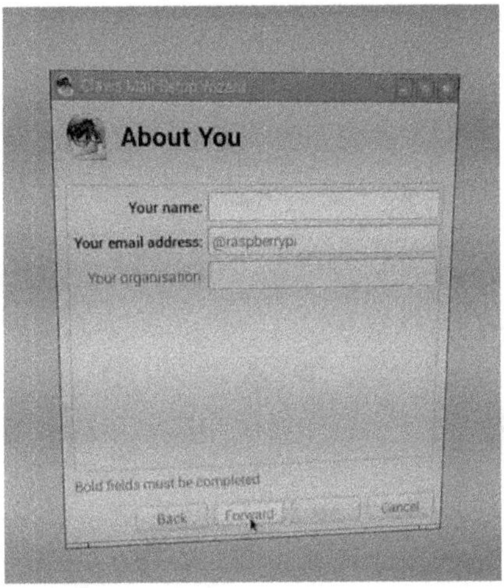

Once filled in you click Forward again and you are led to a window where you fill in information about sending an email.

Fill in then click Forward again and you are led to a window about Receiving email.

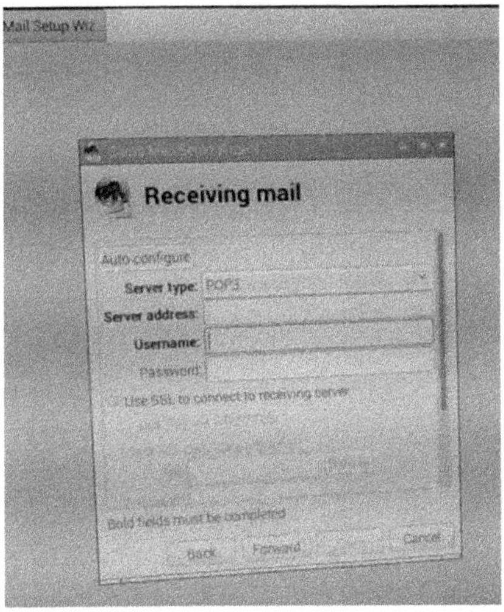

Fill in then click Forward again to get a window requesting the name of the mailbox.

Fill this in then click Forward. This will lead to a window confirming that you have finished installing Claws.

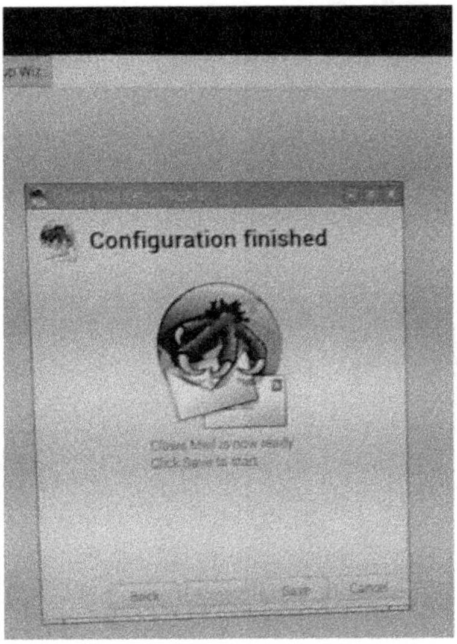

Click Save and you have the completed email client.

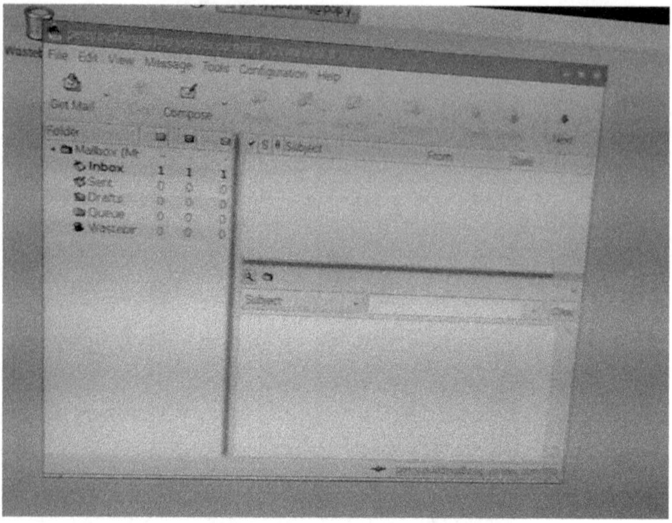

You may find that some tweaks using Preferences, under Configuration, are necessary to get everything running perfectly. Very useful information about Claws can be found at *www.claws-mail.org/ documentation.php*.

Is there another More User-Friendly Email Client?

Fortunately, there is; it is called *Icedove,* and the next few paragraphs will tell you how to get it up and running. In order to do so, it is necessary to do a bit of typing in the terminal which can be obtained using the 4th icon on the top left. If you click on it a black window appears as described in the previous chapter.

In the last chapter, you were able, by some very trivial use of the terminal to get the browser *Firefox.* Using almost identical methods you are going to get a browser that is vastly superior to the Claws, which you were given.

Open your terminal and type in then enter

apt-get install icedove --no-install-recommends

A series of Windows will appear. Fill in all prompts, whether you opt for a new email address, or one you have already. When the program finishes installing you'll have a really good email client; fast, easily adjusted, absolutely marvelous.

Now you've installed both a new email client and *Firefox*, have a look at the Internet menu now. This is what it will look like:

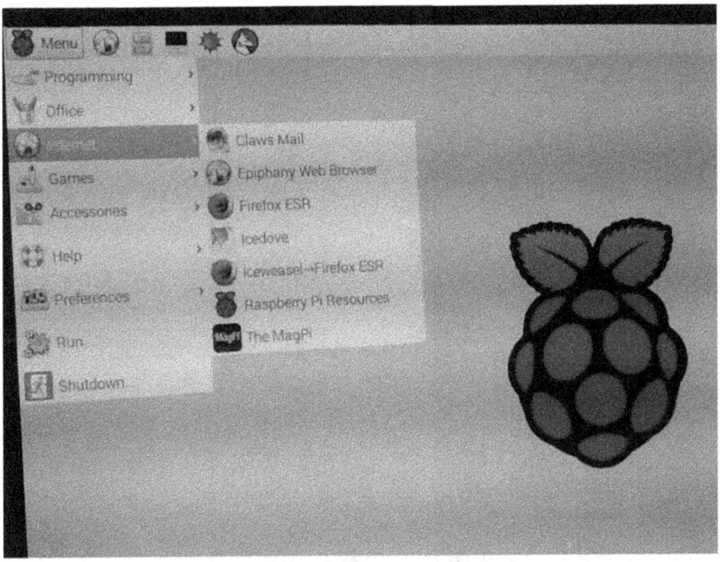

As you can see all the new programs are in the menu.

The old ones are still there, as well.

Other Links on the Internet Menu

Clicking on *Raspberry Pi Resources* leads to a web page:

www.raspberrypi.org/ resources /

which has links to a variety of pages within the *Raspberry Pi* site leading to forums, downloads, help etc.

Clicking on *The MagPi* leads to the online version of *The MagPi* , the official Raspberry Pi magazine. This is a superb magazine and is well worth subscribing to.

If you subscribe to the print version you get a free Raspberry Pi Zero, the version of the Pi, ideal for machines.

Chapter 6

A Media Center Using a Raspberry Pi 3

NOOBS

Install NOOBS from an SD card following the instructions on the NOOBS page. Two XBMC (Xbox Media Center) distributions are included by NOOBS: ELEC and OSMC.

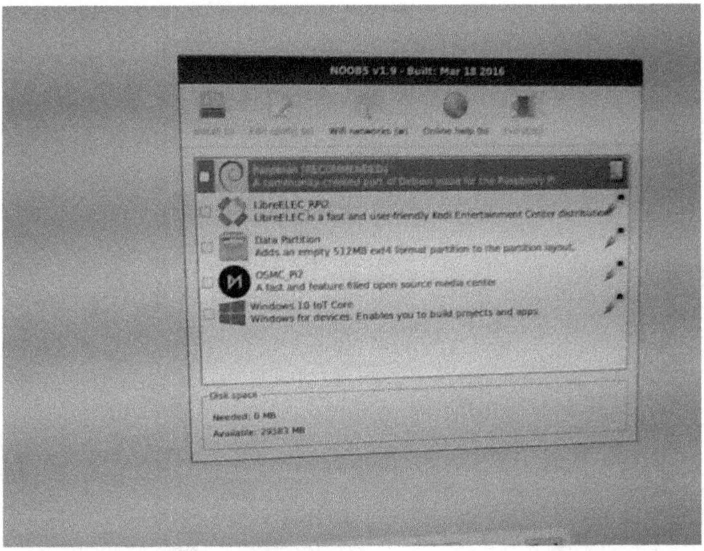

Select **ELEC** or **OSMC** and press the Install button.

You'll be prompted to confirm. This may delete any data on the SD card and you will be warned.

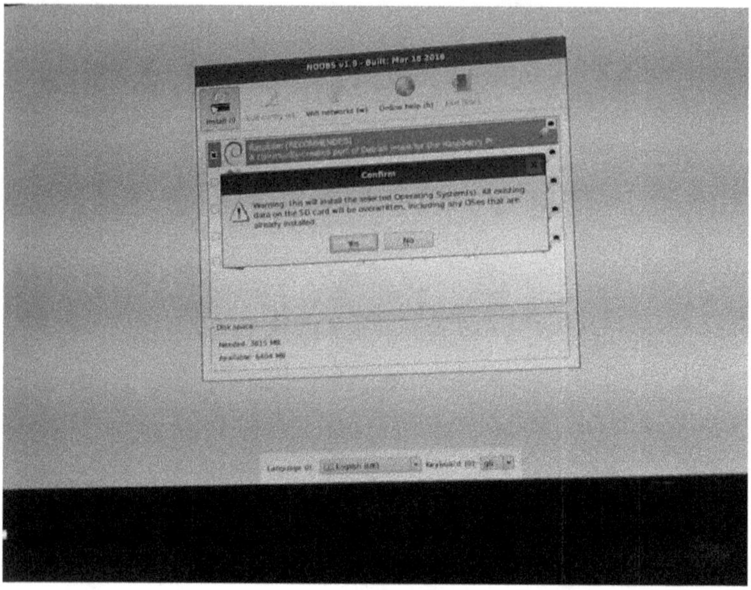

If you're sure, click Yes to continue and start the installation. This will take some time; when it is complete NOOBS will show a window saying: OS(es) Installed Successfully.

Click OK and your Pi will reboot into the distribution you selected. You may be shown a Welcome screen, which will help you configure your setup and help you get started. After answering some questions in what are called *Wizards* you will go to the screens of the media centers.

ELEC

OSMC

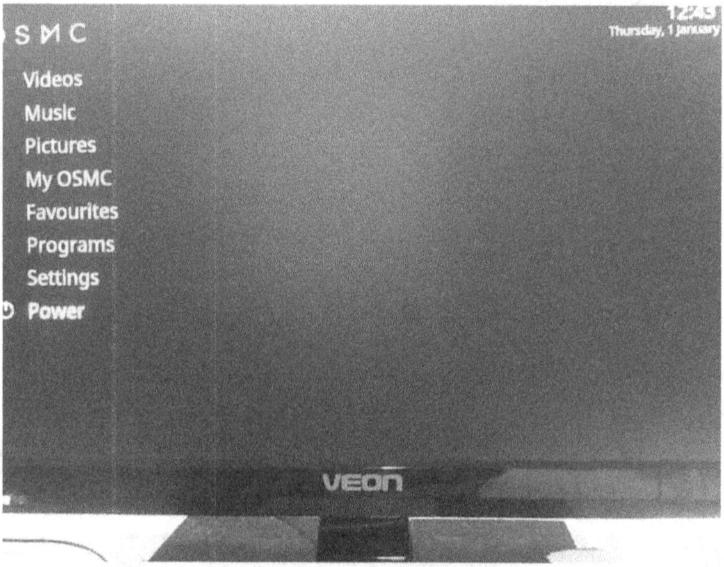

12:43
Thursday, 1 January
Videos
Music
Pictures
My OSMC
Favourites
Programs
Settings
Power
VEON

Using XBMC

Now you've got your XBMC distribution installed you can play media files, configure the system, and install add-ons to add more functionality.

Power

Power can be supplied to the Pi as usual with a USB micro cable; another way, if you are connected to a TV which has a USB port then you can connect the Pi directly with a USB micro cable. The Pi will be switched on when the TV is turned on, and switched off when the TV is turned off.

Control

There are a number of ways this can be achieved; you can use a keyboard and mouse with XBMC, you can use a TV remote with a USB receiver, or use a presentation clicker with directional buttons.

You could use an XBMC app on a smartphone; search for XBMC in the app store of the phone. Configure the app to connect to your XBMC Pi's IP address, once done then use the onscreen remote control or navigate the files from your phone and select what to play.

Playing video and audio files

Copy video and audio files on to your Pi's SD card, or put them on a USB stick or external hard drive. Play these files by choosing *VIDEO* or *AUDIO* in the slider on the main screen, then *Files* to see the inserted media in the list of sources. Select the device and you will be able to navigate it as if you were using a computer. Locate the file, select it then play it.

Connecting a network drive

It is possible to get a connection to a network device such as a NAS (Network Attached Storage) on your local network by using a wired connection. Do this by connecting the Raspberry Pi to your router with an

Ethernet cable. Connect to the device, select *VIDEOS* from the screen and click *Add Videos....*

The *Add Video source* screen will be visible. Select *Browse* then the type of connection. For NAS, choose *Windows network (SMB)*; it will be using the Samba protocol which is an open source version of the Windows file sharing protocol. The device will show if it is on the network. Add this device as a location then you can to navigate through its file system and play its media files.

Settings

XBMC has many options which are configurable. Some of these are: changing screen resolution, choosing a different skin, setting up a screensaver, configuring the file view, and much more. Just go to *SYSTEM* and *Settings* from the main screen.

Add-ons

Add-ons are little programs, usually downloads from the web, you can get that provide extra functionality or enable connection to web services like YouTube. Once you have add-ons you can configure them from the settings menu; a selection is available for you to browse. Select one and you'll be prompted as to how to install it. Each add-on has its own configurations.

AirPlay

AirPlay is owned by Apple and was developed by them to allow wireless streaming between devices of audio, video, and photos. It was originally implemented only in Apple software and devices and was called AirTunes . It was used for audio only. If a speaker is to receive AirPlay then it must be specifically adjusted so it can. The April 2016 issue of MacFormat has an article about how an ordinary speaker can be turned into an AirPlay enabled one by use of a Raspberry Zero.

Both media centers, OSMC, and ELEC , currently make AirPlay possible with the Raspberry Pi 3, however Apple is likely to disallow the current situation in the future as they are very keen that this technology only works on their machines. This would be most unfortunate, however, this may be counter-productive for them as people hate monopolies.

A comparison between OSMC and ELEC

Both OSMC and ELEC are very good media centers, however, in my opinion, ELEC is much more user-friendly. OSMC uses a black line instead of a mouse, I found this quite hard to use. OSMC expects you to use Enter, Escape, and the up and down keys of your keyboard. It is difficult to figure out how to switch off either a song or a video on OSMC while it is quite straightforward on ELEC.

I was guided successfully to an Internet connection when I used ELEC but completely failed such connection with OSMC. Such connection is possible but it is not easily found, certainly not by me. I Googled for a while and found a way it can be done however the method was very inconvenient. In this respect, ELEC is far better.

There are very thoughtful articles at http://www.htpcbeginner.com/openelec-vs-osmc-raspberry-pi/ and http://www.wirelesshack.org/openelec-vs-osmc-on-a-raspberry-pi-model-2-kodi.html, which discuss the merits of both systems. People who are clearly an expert on the merits of media centers wrote them. They make interesting reading.

Summary

Both media centers have much to recommend them. I vastly prefer ELEC however others speak highly of OSMC. Once you have selected one that is right for you then it may well be a good choice to remove the other, particularly if all you require is a station in which to center your media.

Chapter 7

Programming with a Raspberry Pi 3

As well as considering the programming languages, which come with the Raspian Operating System, we will begin with a thorough look at the Libre Office and consider its use.

What is the Libre Office?

Libre Office is a completely free alternative to the well known, but expensive, Microsoft Office. For many people Microsoft Office is the only possible set of tools; word processing means Word, spreadsheet means Excel and presentation means PowerPoint. When it comes to a database many people do not know what a database is and the Microsoft Office database Access is not nearly so well known.

What follows is a program by program comparison of the Offices.

Word Processing

Libre office is largely compatible with Microsoft office and this is particularly true of the word processors. The Libre Office word processor is called Writer while that of Microsoft is, of course, called Word. Both of these are very good. They both have very good features. A grammar checker (some believe Writer's is much better), a solid auto save system, huge support for many different formats and much more. Any document made with Writer can be opened in Word, and vice versa. This means that if you have Writer at home and you took a file that you made with this package somewhere else would you would have no difficulty in opening it in Word, nor would you have any difficulty in opening any Word documents with Writer.

Let us now consider spreadsheets. Excel is the Microsoft spreadsheet and many people think that Excel is the only spreadsheet. They are of course wrong. Libre Office has a spreadsheet program called Calc. Calc can do any sort of ordinary work that is expected from Excel and it's macros can easily be moved over to Exce, but unfortunately it does not work the other way. Microsoft has devised a macro language called VBA (Visual Basic for Applications) which is not easily moved to other applications, such as Calc.

Let us now consider presentation software. Libre Office presentation software is called Impress. Microsoft has done a superb job of publicizing and popularizing their Office and, as with Excel and spreadsheets, many people think that presentation software has to be PowerPoint. In fact Impress is just as good as PowerPoint. It has a huge number of features and can easily do some impressive things such as slides.

The Libre Office database is called Base. It is a very good relational database, somewhat similar to FileMaker. It has all of the features, which you would expect in a modern database such as forms, reports, SQL, and relational table support. Base requires the Java programming language, however that is no problem, as this is in the Raspian operating system.

Programming

Programming languages are depicted as *low* or *high* level. The most fundamental language is machine-code, written using binary, i.e. 1 or 0. It is the lowest level. The *higher* a language is the more meaningful it is to humans.

A higher level language than machine-code, actually utilised by a computer, is *assembly language*. It is regarded as low-level as it is only one level above machine language. It is not in anyway abstract. It is specific to the machine it is on.

Languages such as C#,VBA, Java, or JavaScript allow a programmer to create programs ,which are to a greater or lesser degree independent of the of computer used. Computer languages like this are higher level as they are more like human language, and less like machine languages which are only 0 and 1.

It is far simpler for people to read, write, and maintain programs written in high-level languages than in low-level languages. Despite this programs in high-level languages must be changed into machine-code by a compiler or interpreter.

A table of common computer languages from lowest to highest follows.

Langu age	Machi ne-code	Assem bly	C	C+ +	Ja va	Pyth on	Pe rl	JavaSc ript	Ru by

Compilers, Interpreters, and Assemblers

All programs need conversion to machine-code for the computer to use them. This carried out either by a *compiler*, or by an *interpreter*.

Compilers take an entire program and convert it to machine-code, to produce what is called an *executable* file. Compiled languages include C and C++.

Interpreters do the conversion line by line as the program is converted to machine-code. Among interpreted languages are Perl, JavaScript and Ruby.

Java and Python are different in that they are a mixture of both.

The conversion of assembly languages machine-code is by what is known as an *assembler*.

Control Structures of Computer Programs

These are sequential, selection or conditional, and iterative structures.

The sequential is the default control structure which means it operates unless told otherwise. The computer executes statements line by line, in the order in which they appear. We have already seen this in the chapter on *Bash*, the command line language for the terminal.

The selection or conditional structure is used when a condition is encountered. A sequence of statements is executed depending on whether the condition is true or false. The program has a choice of two or more alternative paths. Condition means any expression or value that returns a Boolean value, meaning true or false.

The main types of selection statements are "if," "if/ else" and "switch" statements. The most common are the "if" and "if/else" statements . Switch statements are used when there are multiple cases with which to make a selection.

The iterative (repetition) structure executes a series of statements repeatedly, given the truth of a condition. In computing languages such controal structures are called *loops*. The most common iterative statements are the "while," "do until" and "for" loops. A loop are described as either *event controlled* or *counter controlled.* Event-controlled loops execute a sequence of statements the occurrence of an event. Counter-controlled loop executes the statements a previously decided number number of times.

Scratch Computing Language

Scratch is a free application that allows the teaching of basic programming concepts in a visual way. It was created by the Lifelong Kindergarten Group at MIT. Scratch was originally for children in the ages from 8 to 17. However its interface allows anyone to learn to program. Scratch is a wonderful introduction to programming. Scratch teaches programming concepts such as. varibles, conditionals and loops however it is not a very powerful programming language. It would be inadvisable to attempt anything serious with Scratch. However, after learning to use it, you can be sure that when you get a language such as Python, Java, Objective-C, JavaScript or PHP you will approach it with confidence.

The next few paragraphs will show how the three fundamental structures of computing languages can be shown with Scratch.

Programming in Scratch

Sequential Structure

Open the Scratch workbench window

The cat is called a *Sprite* . Go the top left of the Scratch workbench and click on the *Motion* button then drag a *move 10 steps* control into the Scripts screen then change the 10 to 100s by clicking on it then typing 100. Now move the control *turn 15 degrees* onto the Scripts screen and change 15 to 1 80. Make sure the two pieces are interlocking. Now click on either of the pieces. The sprite moves 100 and then rotates 180°. One computer command is followed by the other. This is how the sequential structure works.

Conditional Structure

We are going to have to create a variable. Go to the *Variables* button in the top left-hand corner and click on it.

1. A little window comes up in which you are to fill in. Enter a name then decide on whether this variable is specific for all sprites or only just one sprite then click OK or press Enter. A little box with your variable will appear on the

screen. It is usually not necessary and can be deleted by using right-click. My variable is called colorNumber. It is always best to give variables names which are meaningful to the context in which you are working.

2. Now click the *Control* button in the top left corner and drag the structure if/else onto the Scripts panel

3. Go to *Operators* in the top left corner and drag the hexagon with an = on it onto the Scripts panel and place in the hexagonal hole at the top of if/else. Fill it in. I filled in the operator as colorNumber = 0. Click the *Looks* button in the top left corner and drag two *set color effect* controls onto the Scripts panel (iv) Go back to

the top left panel and click *Variables,* get two *set colorNumber* controls get put them into the if /else.

When you have completed this the Scripts screen should look like the diagram below.

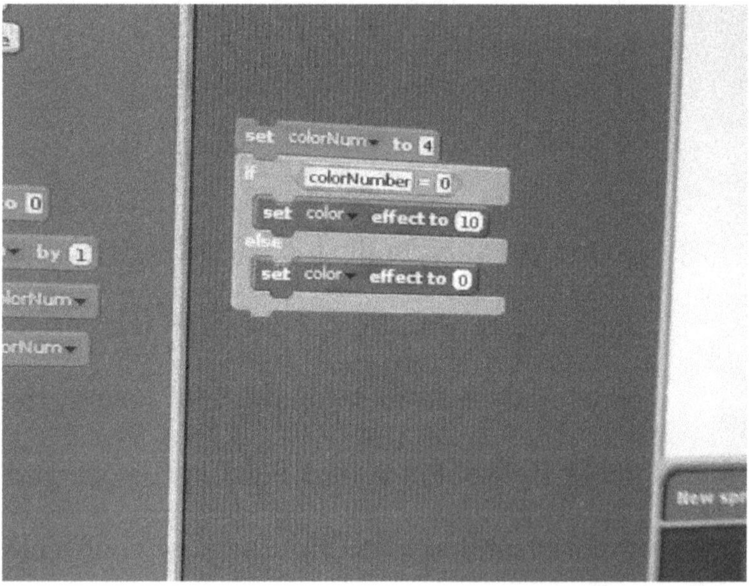

You must save this by pressing ctrl S. By putting different numbers into the *set colorNum* control and clicking on any part of the structure you will see your sprite turning color depending on whether you enter 0 or not into the *colorNum* control. Each time you change the number be sure to ctrl S.

Iterative Structure

Have a look at the two diagrams below, which illustrate an iterative control structure in a program.

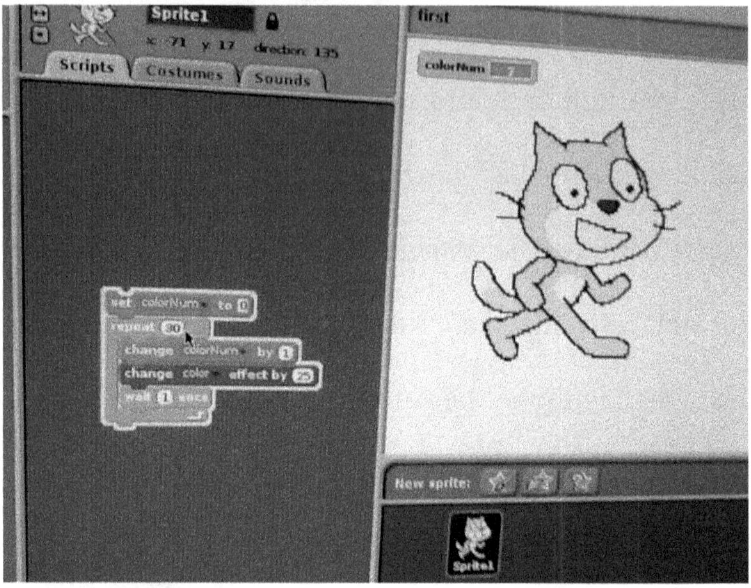
Sprite1
Scripts
Costumes
Sounds
first
colorNum
set colorNum to 0
repeat 30
change colorNum by 1
change color effect by 25
wait 1 secs
New sprite:
Sprite1

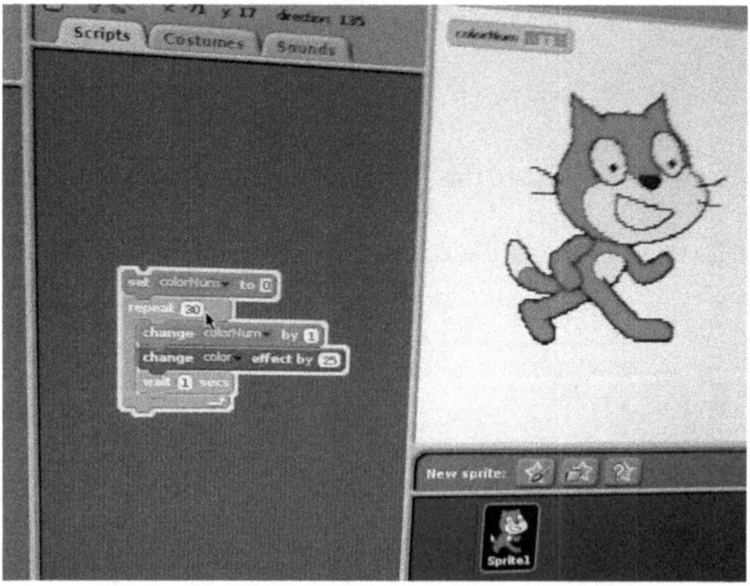
Scripts
Costumes
Sounds
set colorNum to 0
repeat 30
change colorNum by 1
change color effect by 25
wait 1 secs
New sprite:
Sprite1

The structure, which repeats the same commands, is the *repeat 30*.

Basically the program does the following:

(1) A variable called *colorNum* is set to 0;

(2) There are 30 repetitions of:{

(i) *colorNum* being increased by 1;

(ii) The number of the actual color of the sprite being increased by 25}.

The effect of (ii) when the program is run is a little box on the screen showing the increasing value of *colorNum,* and ever-changing colors of the sprite.

When the program stops the value in the little box will be 30.

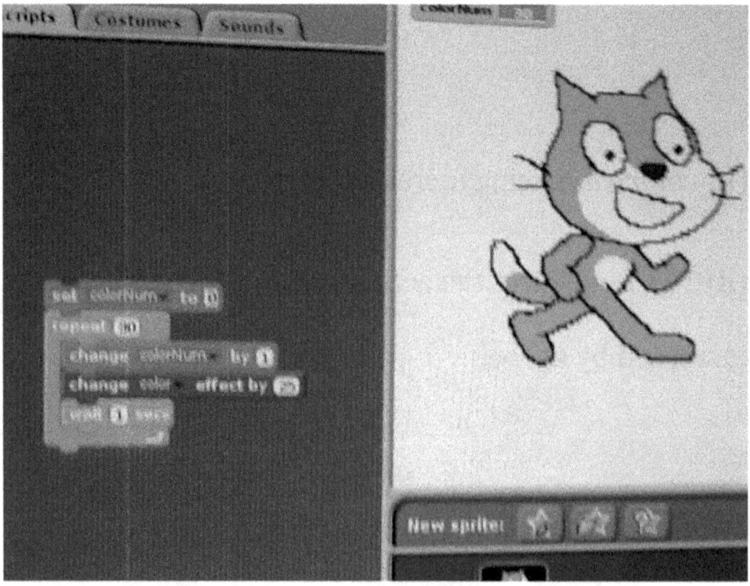

If you need help with your Scratch there is an abundance of resources about it on the web. One of the best can be found at https://scratch.mit.edu/help/videos/.

Programming with Python

Python is a high level, object oriented, scripting language, developed by a man called Guido van Rossum, in the late 1980s and early 1990s, in Holland. Python is very similar to other languages such as C, C++ , Java, JavaScript, Smalltalk and UNIX shell. It is designed to be very understandable and certainly is, if you are familiar with one or more of the languages previously mentioned.

A feature of the Python language is that it relies far more on formatting than many other computer languages . Python is interpreted, which means that it is processed line by line by the interpreter at runtime. This is similar to Perl, JavaScript and PHP. You do not need to compile the program before executing it as with C.

Python is object oriented. This means it supports objects, which encapsulate (have) code within them. It is a very good language for beginner level programs and it supports the developments of a huge variety of applications from simple documents to the most complicated applications, such as those in games and commerce.

If you have a Raspberry Pi 3 then go to the

programming menu.

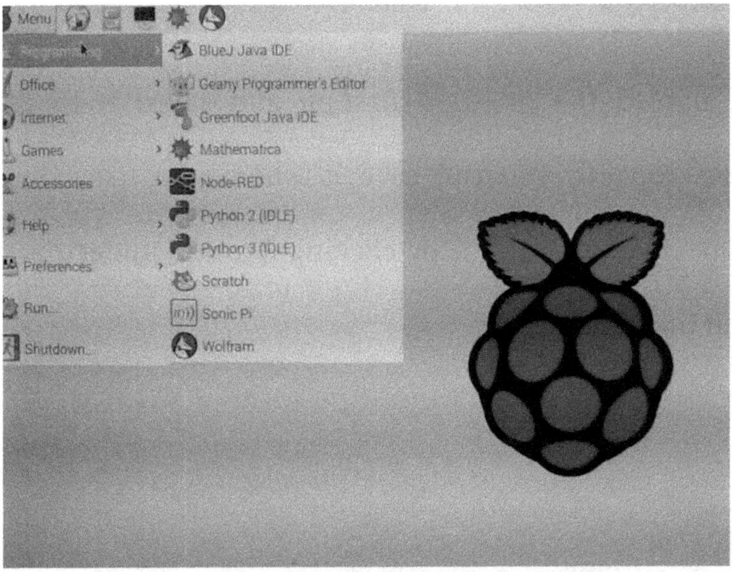

Although two programs called Python are specifically mentioned go to the Geary Programmer's Editor. It makes Python programming very easy.

Type the program below into the editor and save it

with the suffix .py. This is very important. If you don't do this your program will not work.

I named the program *first.py* and saved it to the desktop but you can save it where you like. Once saved you can run it by clicking *Execute* under *Build* on the menu.

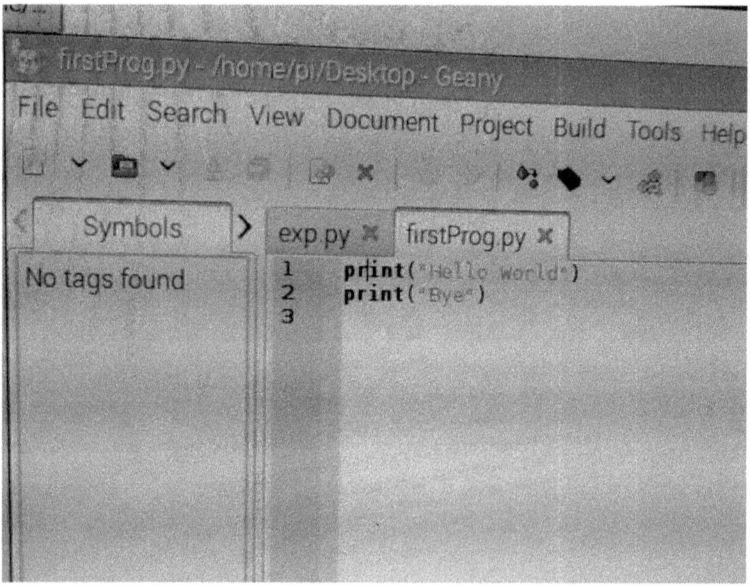

The output appears on a terminal.

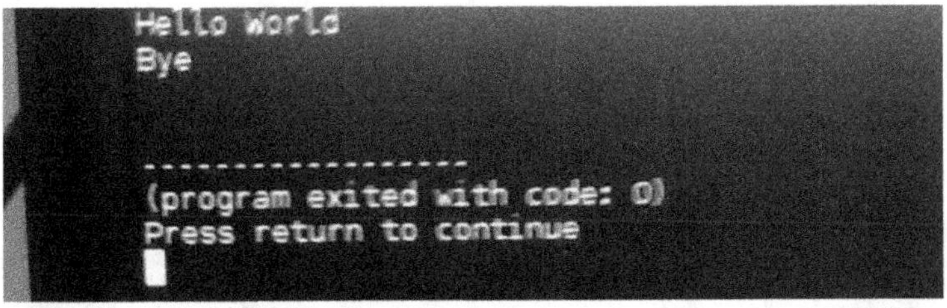

If there is anything wrong the editor has a little red hexagon on the menu

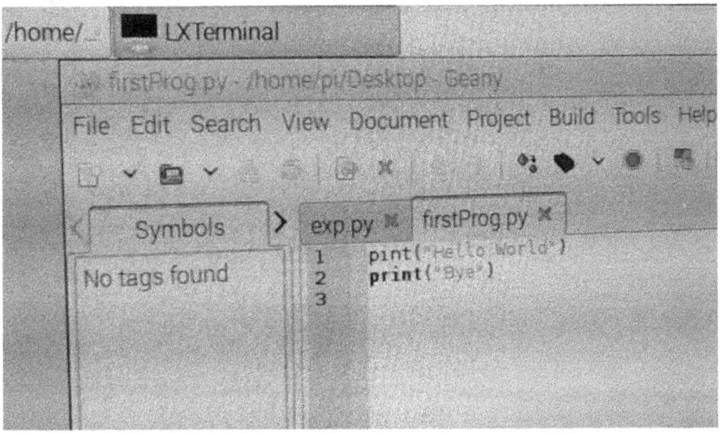

and when you run it the terminal tells you which line the error is in.

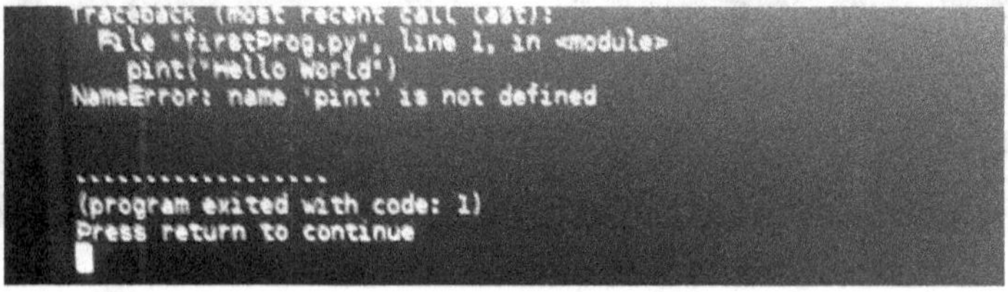
File "firstProg.py", line 1, in <module>
pint("Hello World")
NameError: name 'pint' is not defined
(program exited with code: 1)
Press return to continue

Here, I deliberately misspelt *print* as *pint*.

The program above is one that is purely sequential. The next window shows one, which is sequential but also has a conditional structure in it.

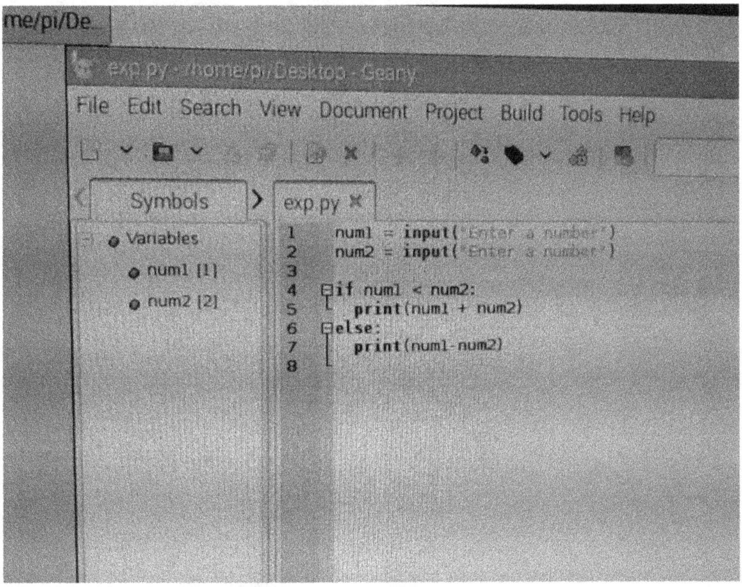

When it is run the output appears as:

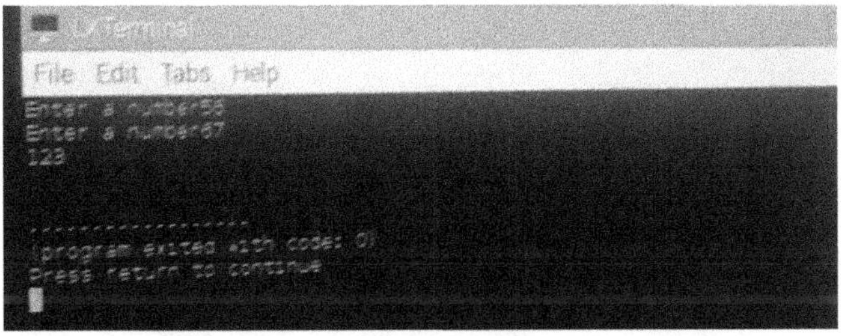

The conditional statement is if num1 < num2: then else:

Notice below each of these the writing was indented (further from left margin). This is the main way that Python separates blocks of code. It is different to C++, JavaScript and VBA.

We will continue this brief examination of Python by having a look at a program that uses an iterative structure.

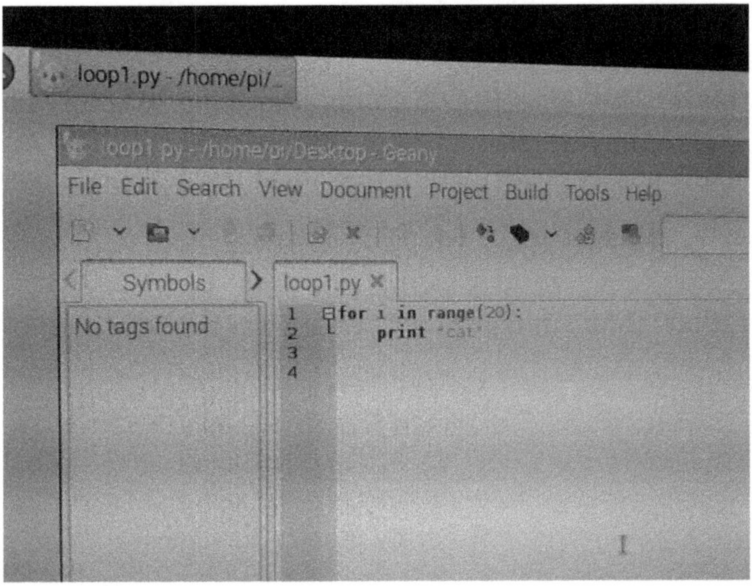

Here is the output.

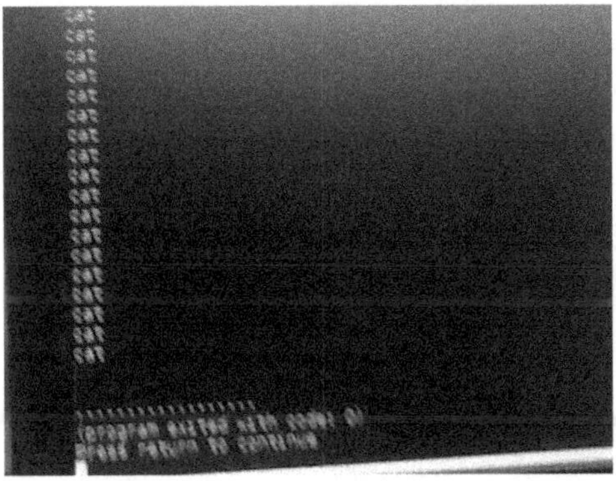

All the program does is print the word "cat" twenty times. The way in which an iterative structure is achieved is markedly different from that of C++, Java or JavaScript; these all use {} to enclose blocks of code rather than indentations which is the method of Python.

We fill finish this brief description of Python by having a look at a program that creates a class then uses an object from that class.

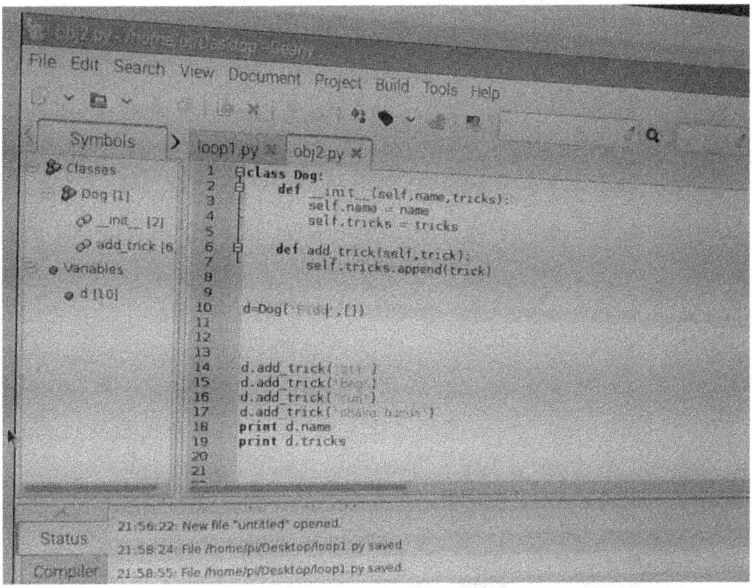

The program first creates a *class* called *Dog* which has two *attributes*. These are *name* and *tricks*. The attribute *tricks* is an array into which tricks will be added. There is a *method* of the class called *add_trick*. The program then creates an object called *d* from the class of *Dog* with the name *Fido* and it adds four tricks to Fido's repertoire which are 'sit', 'beg', 'run' and 'shake hands'. Finally the program prints the name and the tricks.

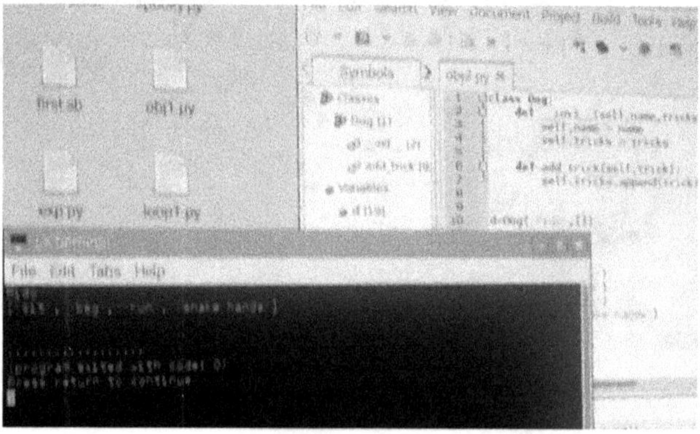

Unlike Scratch, which has no purpose beyond being a teaching tool, Python is a very useful language, applied widely. I have given but a glimpse of the things you can do with it.

There is a wealth of material such as videos and tutorials on the Internet if you want to expand your knowledge of this powerful language.

Alternatively, if you are interested in Python, consider picking up my book, "Python Programming: Learn Python Programming In A Day - A Comprehensive Introduction To The Basics Of Python & Computer Programming" available in ebook or print via Amazon here: www.amazon.com/dp/B01GULF8I6

Programming with Java

There are two Java Integrated Development Environments (IDE) on the programming menu.

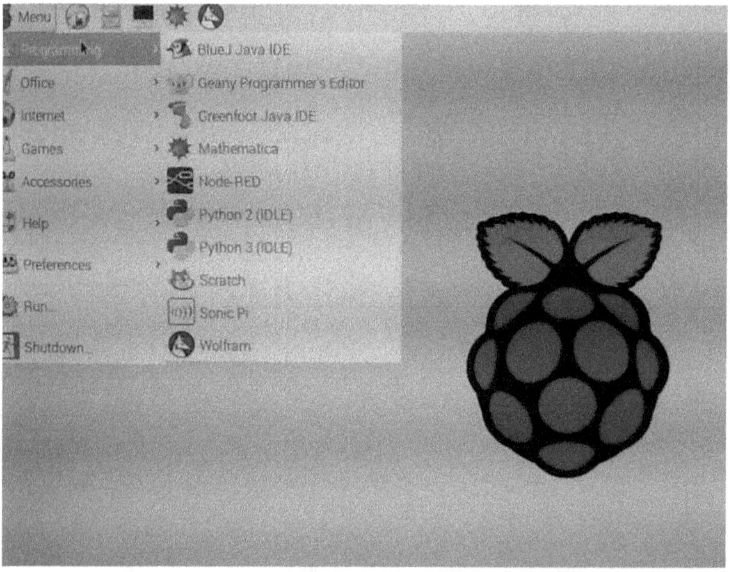

Let's open the BlueJ IDE.

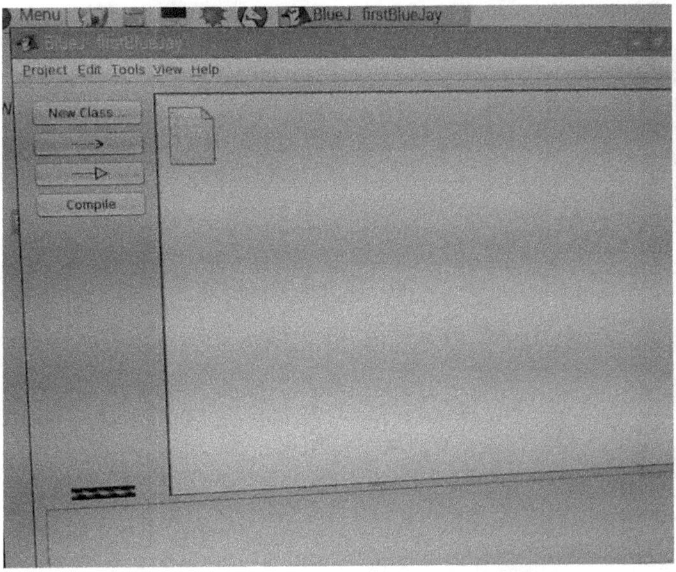

Java is completely object oriented and you work exclusively with classes. Your first move will to click *New Class*

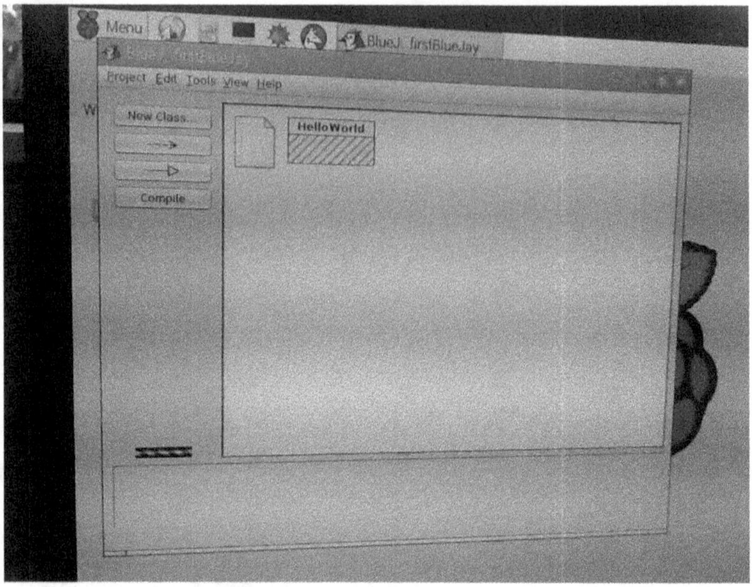

There are a lot of tutorials which show you how to proceed. One of the best series is at https://www.youtube.com/watch?v=UMcijMC4Dwk.

Another is https://www.cs.utexas.edu/users/scottm/cs307/handouts/BlueJProjectInstructions.html.

Now let's open the Greenfoot IDE

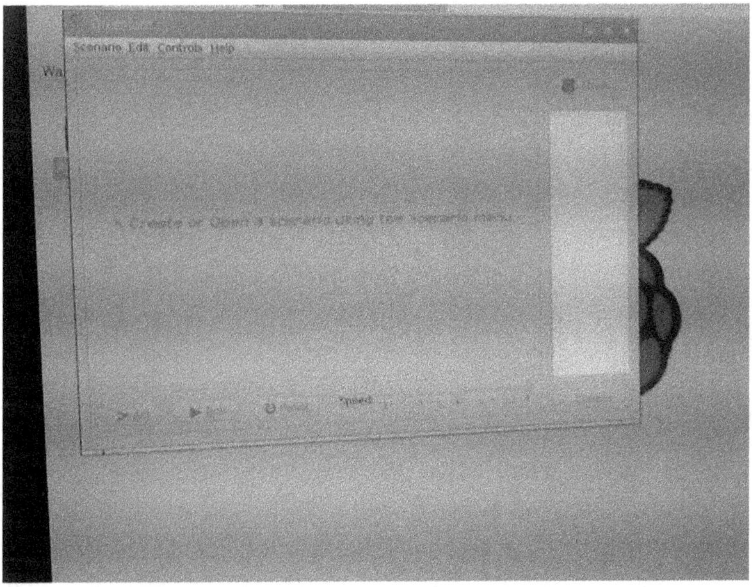

There are very good tutorials designed to show you how to use this. A very good series of videos is at https://www.youtube.com/watch?v=NcGe141R2yA

If you prefer a written tutorial then have a look at http://www.oracle.com/webfolder/technetwork/tutorials/OracleAcademy/GreenfootSelfStudyV1/obe.html

Which is best BlueJ or Greenfoot? If you are a reasonably experienced programmer then BlueJ is probably better for you, but if you are fairly new to programming then Greenfoot is more suitable. Java is more complicated than Python, JavaScript or VBA so in choosing a language to learn programming with, once you have mastered Scratch, then one of Python or JavaScript would be a sensible choice.

Now let's have a look at the remaining couple of options on the programming menu: Mathematica and Sonic. Let us start with Mathematica.

What is Mathematica?

Mathematica is a very powerful program, originally designed for education, but whose uses now extend far beyond the classroom. Mathematica is a software package that can do calculations, draw graphs, and do mathematical modeling and statistics. It is a program that can address complex mathematical ideas that arise in fields from research to industry.

The possible uses of Mathematica are virtually boundless, you are limited only by your imagination. It is a perfect tool with which to study new mathematical questions. Mathematica is often used to explore subjects such as calculus, differential equations and statistics. Mathematica gives the ability to perform calculations that would be impossible using paper and pencil. Mathematica is able to perform symbolic algebraic calculations. Mathematica can also model in a variety of ways from simple two-dimensional plots to three-dimensional color animations. Mathematica can answer a question like, "What is the integral of the cos(x)?". Mathematica has all the information in it which is on the Wolfram alpha site.

Mathematica was developed by Steven Wolfram, who was on the faculty of the university of Illinois. He started work on it in 1986 and released it in 1988. It has had many upgrades since then.

The Mathematica language is quite different to languages like Python and JavaScript. The best way to master it, as for anything, is practice. The following website is a rich source of examples: https://www.wolfram.com/language/gallery/

If you go to this site you will be amazed at what Mathematica has been applied to. Among the questions it can answer are: how do you make a logo design, hiding secrets messages in images, plotting the yearly path of the sun, recognizing handwritten text, interpreting natural language, generating random pronounceable words, determining if a text is prose or poetry, determining the author of a text, determining the language of a text, classifying images as either day or night, making a map of population distributions, making flag maps, plotting the population growth of a country, blurring faces in pictures and many others.

When I wrote this book I had never used Mathematica , however with a few Google questions I was able to find how to solve the equation $x^2 - 4x + 3 = 0$.

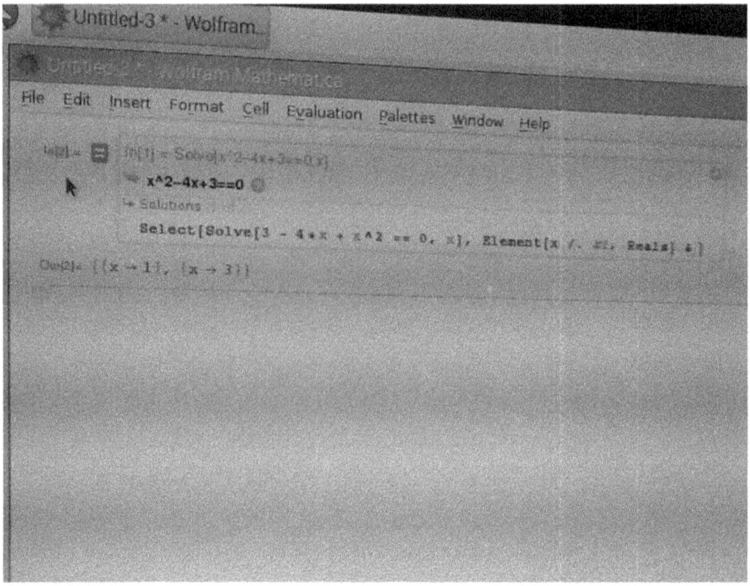

Using a Mathematica notebook I entered In[1] := Solve[x^2 - 4x + 3 ==0,x] and pressed [Enter]. A short time later after Mathematica had done its calculations the answers $x = 1$ and $x = 3$ appeared as

Ou[2] = {{ x --> 1 }{ x --> 3}}.

Next, I did some integration from calculus.

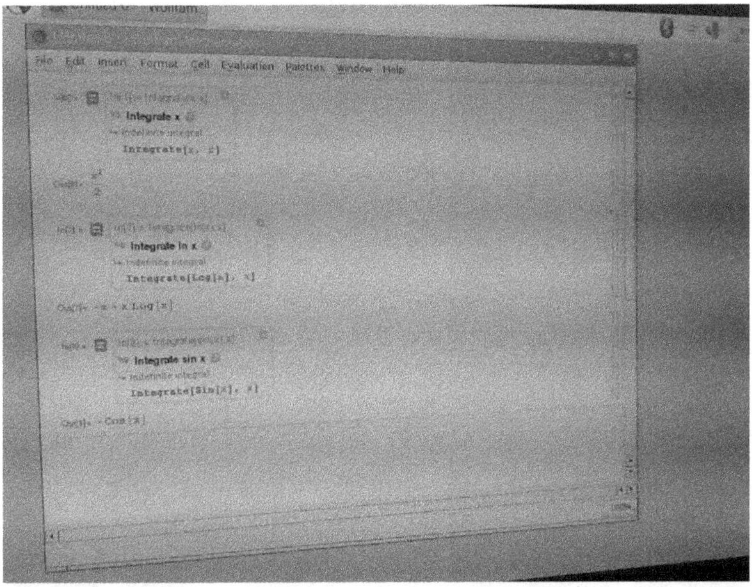

Using a Mathematica notebook I entered In[1] := Integrate[x,x] and pressed [Enter]. A short time later after Mathematica had done its calculations the

answers as Ou[2] $\frac{x^2}{2}$.

I drew the graph of the parabola $y = x^2$.

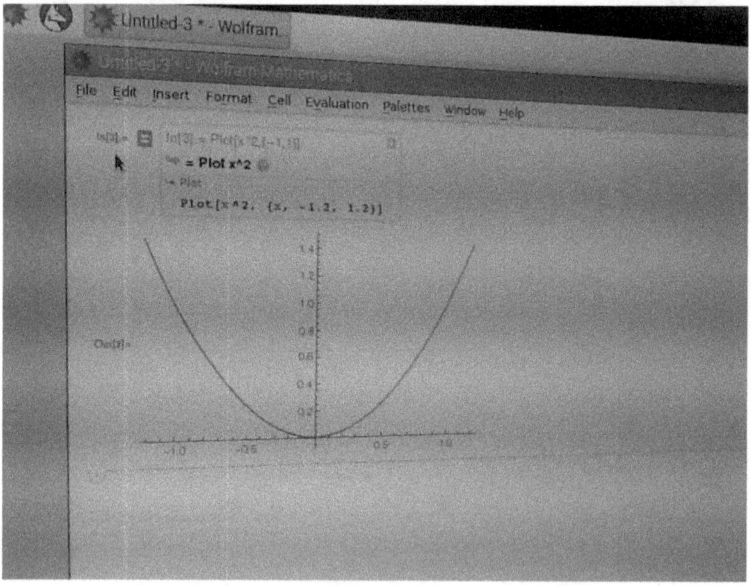

Using a Mathematica notebook I entered In[2] := Plot[x62 ,{-1,1}] and pressed [Enter]. A short time later after Mathematica had done its calculations the answers as Ou[2] which was the graph above.

The examples I have given are very simple but they illustrate the power of this application.

The final item in the Programming menu is called *Sonic Pi.*

What is Sonic Pi?

Sonic Pi is an open source-programming environment developed with the computer language Ruby by Sam Aaron. It teaches programming concepts through the process of creating sound. There is a scheme of work that emphasizes the importance of creativity in the process of learning, and gives users the opportunity to turn their sonic ideas into reality. The scheme of work is specifically targeted towards introductory computer science courses. It has been developed to be in line with the new computing curriculum in the UK. The scheme of work is the result of a close collaboration between computing teachers and researchers at the University of Cambridge. It has been trialed with great success at a variety of schools.

Go to the programming menu and click on *Sonic Pi*

After a short while the diagram above appears. This changes into the diagram.

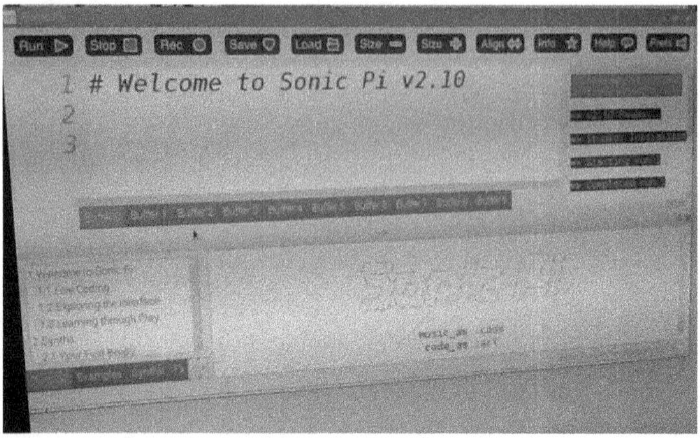

The actual scheme of work is in the bottom left hand panel. If you click 1.1 and follow the instructions given you get this.

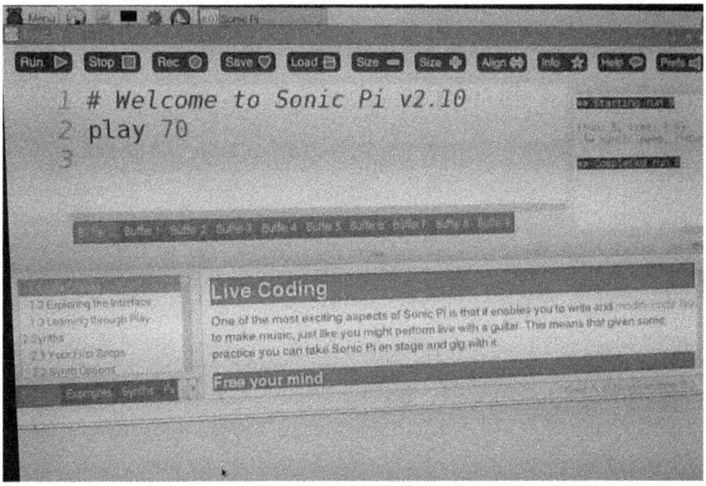

Just follow the course in the left panel. If you need extra instruction then watch this very good video: https://www.youtube.com/watch?v=ixn6d4qSK5I

The presenter does a superb job of showing the basics of *Sonic Pi* and in generating enthusiasm for this.

There is one other option on the programming sub-menu and that is *Node-Red*. This is concerned with the programming of real life programs, and will be considered in the last chapter.

Chapter 8

Interacting with the Physical World using a Raspberry Pi 3

Steve case was the CEO and founder of AOL. It was a company that dominated the Internet in the 90s. This company was so successful that they merged with Time-Warner. In his brilliant book, *The Third Wave*, Steve described how computing could be described as having developed in three waves.

The building of the infrastructure and the foundations of the industry dominated the first wave. Prominent in this were such well-known names as Hewlett-Packard, Microsoft, Apple, AOL and much more. The pioneers needed to lower the cost of connection, which used to be as high this $10. They had to beg computer companies to build modems into their computers. Case describes how in AOL much work had to be done explaining what the Internet was and how it worked.

The second wave began at the beginning of the 21st century, inflating the dot-com bubble, and helping it burst. The second wave was concerned with building on top of the Internet, which was now well established. Search engines are a good example of the thing that the second wave involved. It is now possible to get all of the information, which is on the Internet, with search engines like Google. Another feature of this wave are the social networks like Facebook, Twitter, and Linked-In which let people organize themselves.

The second wave has software as a service. However, the second wave is giving way to a new thing. We are moving from the Internet to the Internet of Things (IoT) where many devices are connected and converse with each other. The Raspberry Pi is particularly suited for developments in this era.

The Internet of Things will be very important in healthcare. Soon people will have apps that track their vital signs and produce data that doctors can use. People who use the Raspberry Pi will probably build many of these apps.

The IoT is already, and will be more important in education. New technology will enable teachers and parents to interact in ways, which have never been seen before. Some of these are virtual tutors, tablets which replace textbooks and adjust to students learning styles, new real-time assessments.

Another area, which the Internet of things will be involved in, is food. Involvement with it offers great opportunities to the inventor equipped with a Raspberry Pi. Food inspection and packaging will be completely revolutionized. Stoves and refrigerators will be more sensitive and aware of their contents. They will warn when food is stale or putrid.

The third wave is cresting. The Raspberry Pi is an ideal tool for those who wish to exploit and ride this wave and take advantage of the many openings in this rapidly growing field that have now become apparent.

A fascinating blog about this, https://www.raspberrypi.org/blog/getting-started-with-iot/, can be found on the Pi site. In it is described a people counter which uses only one extra piece of equipment; this is a passive infra-red sensor. Unlike other topics in this book the purchase of extra equipment is almost mandatory. The next few paragraphs will deal with a couple of pieces of such equipment.

Breadboard

A breadboard is a very useful device for prototyping circuits. It allows you to easily plug in and remove components and so if there are going to be many changes or if you just want to make a circuit quickly, it will be much quicker than soldering up your circuit.

One of the features of IoT computing is the development and experimentation with electric circuits. The commercial way of doing this is via soldering, a process which is messy, and can be dangerous for the inexperienced.

A breadboard to quickly try out and change circuits is vital so the purchase of a breadboard is almost mandatory.

Touch Screen

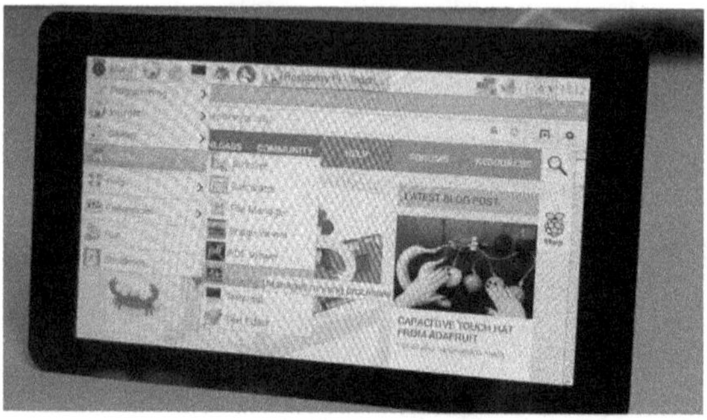

Touch screens are a rugged means of display of important information. Some amazing IoT devices have been made with these.

Camera

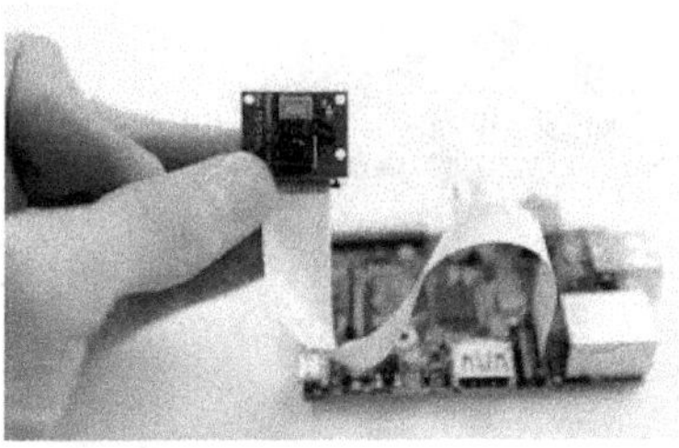

Another device that has been created for IoT purposes and the Raspberry Pi is a tiny camera. The possible uses are limited only by the imagination of the user. This diagram shows such a camera combined with a Raspberry Pi to make a surveillance camera

Raspberry Pi Zero

No discussion of the Raspberry Pi and the IoT would be complete without mention of the Raspberry Pi Zero which is the stripped down version of the Pi, ideal for putting into devices.

The previous four paragraphs have described a few of pieces of hardware which you can purchase in order to begin your exploration of IoT. We now turn our attention to the software available for the Pi.

Node - Red

Node-Red in its simplest form is an open source visual editor for wiring the Internet of Things which was developed by IBM. What this means is that it is software for making devices exchange information without concern about interfacing code.

The system has Nodes which appear as icons that are dragged and dropped onto a canvas and joined together. Each Node has different functionality.

Programs which normally would have hours to complete are done in a few minutes. But with Node-Red a good programmer is able to do it in minutes. Node-Red does the hard work.

Node-Red is available on the Raspian Programming Menu.

Node-Red Tutorials

There are many sites on the Internet, which give information, and training on this powerful application. Among them are:

https://github.com/rwaldron/johnny-five/wiki/Getting-started-with-Raspberry-Pi-node-red-and-IoT

https://developer.ibm.com/recipes/tutorials/deploy-watson-iot-node-on-raspberry-pi/

http://logic.sysbiol.cam.ac.uk/teaching/jamred.pdf

http://nodered.org/docs/hardware/raspberrypi

Windows 10 IoT

Microsoft has realized how important the IoT is and has put their technology on NOOBS to be used by people using the Raspberry Pi 3 to develop IoT applications. The reviews of it are very critical and see the aims of the Raspberry Foundation, with its high ideals and generous ways, to be the complete opposite of those of Microsoft. The reader is advised to try this offering and see if it is any good for themselves.

Windows 10 IoT Tutorials

There are some sites where there is information. Among them are:

https://developer.microsoft.com/en-us/windows/iot

https://blogs.windows.com/buildingapps/2015/08/10/hello-windows-10-iot-core/

http://blog.chrisbriggsy.com/Beginners-guide-to-GPIO-Win10-IoT-Core-Insider-Preview/

Conclusion

The Raspberry Pi 3 provides a wonderful tool for so many different purposes, and is particularly useful for educators teaching computer hardware and innovators in the third wave.

However that doesn't mean anyone else would not benefit by learning how to use this wonderful little machine. I highly recommend it!

Good luck!

A message from the author,

Steve Gold

To show my appreciation for your support, Id like to

offer you a couple of exclusive free gifts:

FREE BONUS!

As a free bonus, I've included a preview of some of my other best-selling books directly after this section. Enjoy!

Thank you again for your support.

Steve Gold

FREE BONUS!: Preview Of **"Arduino: Getting Started With Arduino: The Ultimate Beginner's Guide"**!

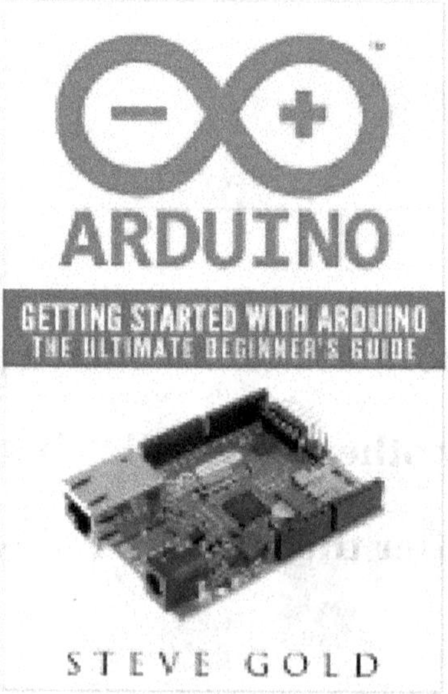
ARDUINO
GETTING STARTED WITH ARDUINO
THE ULTIMATE BEGINNER'S GUIDE
STEVE GOLD

If you enjoyed this book, I have a little bonus for you; a preview of one of my other books "**Arduino: Getting Started With Arduino: The Ultimate**

Beginner's Guide". In this book, I'll show you just how incredible Arduino is, as well as how to complete your first Arduino project. Enjoy the free sample, and feel free to click on the purchase link below if you would like to learn more!

Introduction

If are you fascinated by the simplest of technology, and often wonder about the inner workings of the electronic devices that are ubiquitous in our daily lives, you are likely to find joy in experimenting and tinkering with Arduino.

At the core of everything that comes to life at a flick of a switch – the Christmas tree lights that blink in multiple colors, the apps that open up on a touch screen device, and the microwave oven that heats up your food etc. – is a micro-controller, programmed to perform certain feats when activated. Arduino is an open-source platform that consists of a micro-controller and programming software. Unlike most platforms, Arduino was geared towards non-electricians who want to get creative with electronics, while also being flexible enough to accommodate engineering experts. It is meant to be accessible, low cost and easy to learn, regardless of your previous knowledge in electronics and programming.

This guide will not make you an Arduino expert overnight – in fact, nothing can. What you will learn from this book however are the fundamentals of this amazingly versatile platform, and you'll also have the opportunity to get a firsthand feel for what it can do. You will be guided through the key features of an Arduino circuit board, technical requirements to begin working, how to kick-start your first Arduino, important lingo you'll need to know in order to get by, and how to proceed further in order to keep building upon what you have learnt.

The information here is intended for the absolute beginner in electronics, circuitry and programming. If you have always wanted to learn how to build cool stuff with electronics yet are completely at loss as to how to get started, you now have all the information you'll need at your fingertips in order to make your entry into the exciting world of Arduino. The rest is up to you!

Chapter 1

Understanding Arduino

In 2005, the Ivrea Interaction Design Institute in Italy started a project of creating an open-source platform to be used for building various electronic projects, known as Arduino. Originally geared towards students with little to no background in electronics or computer programming, the platform eventually gained worldwide popularity due to its accessibility and beginner-friendly features.

Over the years since its inception, Arduino has garnered the attention and enthusiasm of hobbyists, artists, programmers, students and even hackers from all levels of experience. Being an open-source platform, it continues to grow with contributions from a diverse community of users that keep pushing the limits of its capabilities. In fact, Arduino has been the backbone behind thousands of projects and applications, from everyday objects to complex scientific equipment.

The Arduino platform consists of two components:

1. **The hardware** – A physical programmable circuit board, also known as the microcontroller. There are different types of Arduino boards (more on this in Chapter 2).

2. **The Software** – The Integrated Development Environment (IDE) that runs on the computer, used for writing and uploading programming codes to the physical board.

Why Go Arduino?

Practically anyone can use Arduino. Experts are sure to have fun with building projects and sharing ideas with other users at online communities. For those with no experience with circuits and micro-controller programming, the platform is excellent for learning and experimenting. However, it is recommended that before exploring the wonders of Arduino, you should at least have a firm understanding of these fundamental concepts:

- The basics of electricity and circuitry
- Voltage, current, resistance and Ohm's law
- Polarity
- Integrated circuits (ICs)
- Digital logic
- Analog versus Digital
- Basic computer programming

What makes Arduino a favorite among amateurs and experts alike is that, compared to other platforms and systems, it simplifies the process of working with micro-controllers. For a start, loading new codes to the board can simply be done with a USB cable, unlike previous programmable circuit boards where a separate piece of hardware has to be used. It is also a plus point that Arduino boards are relatively inexpensive compared to other micro-controller platforms, with some pre-assembled modules costing less than $50. If those perks are not enough, here are some more reasons why Arduino is the platform to go for:

- **Cross-platform** – Arduino's IDE runs on Windows, Macintosh OSX, and Linux operating systems, whereas most micro-controller systems are only compatible with Windows.

- **Simple programming environment** – The Arduino IDE uses a simplified version of C++, making it easier for beginner to learn how to program, yet flexible enough for advance users to get creative and ambitious with.

- **Open source and extensible hardware** – Arduino board plans are published under a Creative Common license, allowing circuit designers to create their own version of the module, extending it and improving upon it.

- **Open source and extensible software** – The Arduino IDE is published as open source tools that experienced programmers can expand on, through C++ libraries. You can also learn the AVR-C programming language from Arduino, just as you can also add AVR-C code directly into Arduino programs.

- **Backed by a supportive community** – If you are absolutely new to the platform and don't know where to begin, there is a wealth of information to be found online due to the popularity of Arduino. You will never run out of resources to learn from, and you can even find pre-coded projects to work on right away (See Chapter 5 for Arduino resources).

What can Arduino do for You?

Arduino was designed with the creative and innovative in mind, regardless of experience level. Artists, designers, electricians, engineers, programmers and science enthusiasts can use it to create interactive objects and environments. Among the things Arduino can interact with include motors, speakers, LEDs, GPS units, cameras, TVs, smart-phones and even the internet.

With Arduino, one can build low cost scientific instruments, do programming for robotics, build interactive prototypes of architectural designs and create installations for musical instruments to experiment with sound, build new video game hardware – and this is just the tip of the iceberg! So, whether your project entails building a robot, a heating blanket, a festive lighting display or a fortune-telling machine, Arduino can serve as a base for your electronic projects.

FREE BONUS!: Preview Of **"Python Programming: Learn Python Programming In A Day - A Comprehensive Introduction To The Basics Of Python & Computer Programming"**

THE COMPLETE BEGINNERS GUIDE TO
PYTHON
PROGRAMMING
LEARN PYTHON PROGRAMMING IN A DAY
PY

If you enjoyed this book, I have a little bonus for you; a preview of one of my other books "**Python Programming: Learn Python Programming In A Day - A Comprehensive Introduction To The Basics Of Python & Computer Programming**". In this book, I'll show you EACTLY how you can get started with Python programming! Enjoy the free sample, and feel free to click on the purchase link below if you would like to learn more!

Introduction

The open-source, high-level programming language, Python, which was developed by Guido van Possum back in the late 80's uses an easy-to-learn yet concise syntax which is perfect for those who are aiming to develop complex code in as short a time as possible.

While the idea of learning Python programming may at first seem like a daunting task, with the right guidance you'll be up and running in no time, whether you're new to Python or new to programming entirely! In this wonderfully easy to follow guide, we've stripper away the filler to make things as simple as possible for the beginner to take their first steps into the world of Python. The information is presented clearly, in an easy-to-follow, step-by-step manner with the aim of minimizing the chances of confusion, while providing the reader with all of the essential information they'll require.

Are you ready to take your first steps towards mastering Python? Let's get started!

Chapter One

Preparing Your Programming Environment

When it comes to installing Python, you might not have to if you have a version of Linux installed on your computer. If you'd like to check to see if you have python installed, you can open your start menu and type 'python' into the search box. If nothing comes up, then you need to install it.

There are a few different operating systems out there, so let's go over how to install Python on each one of them.

Installing Python on Windows

You can visit https://www.python.org/downloads/ in order to download the most recent version of Python. The installation is just like any other Windows software. Just be sure you check the option Add Python 3.5 to PATH while installing.

To change your install location, click on the Customize installation option and click Next. Then enter C: \python35 as the install location.

If it's not checked, then check the Add Python to environment variables.

You can select to install the Launcher for every user on the computer or not, it doesn't really matter, unless someone else plans on using the language, too. Launcher will be utilized to shift between diverse versions of Python that's installed, too.

If your path wasn't set right, then follow these steps in order to fix it. Otherwise, you go on to Running Python Prompt on Windows.

DOS Prompt

If you'd like to use Python from the Windows command line or the DOS prompt, then you have to set the PATH variable correctly.

For Windows 2000, 2003, and XP, click on the Control Panel, go to System, click on Advanced, and then go into Environment Variables. Then click on the variable name PATH. Select Edit and add C:\Python35 to the end of what is already currently there. Of course, use the right directory name.

For Windows Vista, click the Start button and choose the Control Panel. Click System and you will see a section that talks about viewing basic information about the computer and on the left you will see a list of tasks, the last of which will be Advanced system settings. Click on that.

The Advanced tab will be shown, so click on Environment Variables on the bottom right. In the lower box, that's titled System Variables, scroll down to Path and click on the Edit button. Change your path appropriately.

Restart the computer.

For Windows 7 and 8, you have to right click on the Computer from the desktop and select Properties or click Start and choose the Control Panel – System and

Security – System. Click on the Advanced system settings on your left and click on the Advanced button. Click on Environment Variables at the bottom and under the System variables, you have to look for the PATH variable. Then select and press Edit.

Go to the end of the line and put in the appropriate folder name. Click OK and you're finished!

Running Python Prompt on Windows

For those who are using Windows, you can run your interpreter in the command line if you've set the PATH variable right. To open the terminal, click the start button and then just click Run. In the dialog box, type in cmd and press the enter key. Then, type python and ensure there aren't any errors.

Installing Python on Mac OS X

For those who are running Mac OS X, you'll want to use Homebrew, and install python 3. To verify, open your terminal by pressing Command+Space to open the Spotlight search. Type in Terminal and press the enter key. Now, run python 3 and ensure there are not any errors.

Installation on Linux

For those who are using Linux, use your distribution package manager in order to install Python 3. For example, Debian and Ubuntu users should put *sudo apt-get update && sudo apt-get install python 3* in their terminal.

To verify, open it up by pressing Alt and F2 and entering gnome-terminal. If it doesn't work, then refer back to the documentation for the Linux type you have. Run to make sure there are not any errors.

Installing the Python Text Editor

You can't type all your text into the command prompt to run a program because you'd have to do it every time. You need a compiler that's going to read Python for you and you'll need a text editor, but using Notepad on Windows is a very bad idea. It's going to get messy and sometimes it just doesn't work.

There are three editors that are recommended. These are:

PyCharm

Vim

Emacs

You can go to their respective websites and follow their instructions for downloading them. Once you have them open, you can begin your first program!

Your First Program

You might be thinking, uh oh, not again, but the Hello World program is the first program that every programmer learns to run because it teaches you the very basics of programming in any language. Besides, for those who are doing this for the first time in any language, it's pretty exciting!

Open your editor and open up a new file and call it hello.py. Type in this:

print("hello world")

Save the file where you now you're going to remember it and be sure it's in its own folder with your programs.

To run the program:

Open the terminal window.

Change directory to where you saved your file.

Run the program by entering the command hello.py in your command line. The output will be a box that says 'hello world' in it!

Python programs are made up of statements. In your first program, you have only one statement. In this statement, you call the print *statement* to which you supply the text 'hello world.'

In the next chapter, we're going to take a look at the basics of a python program!

Check Out My Other Books!

Elon Musk - The Biography Of A Modern Day Renaissance Man

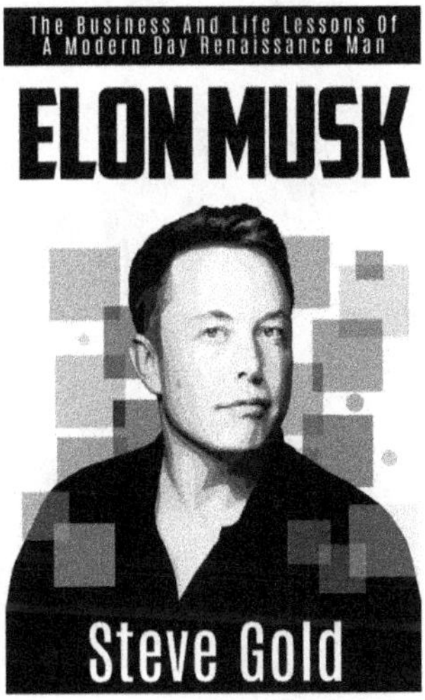

Elon Musk - The Business & Life Lessons Of A Modern Day Renaissance Man

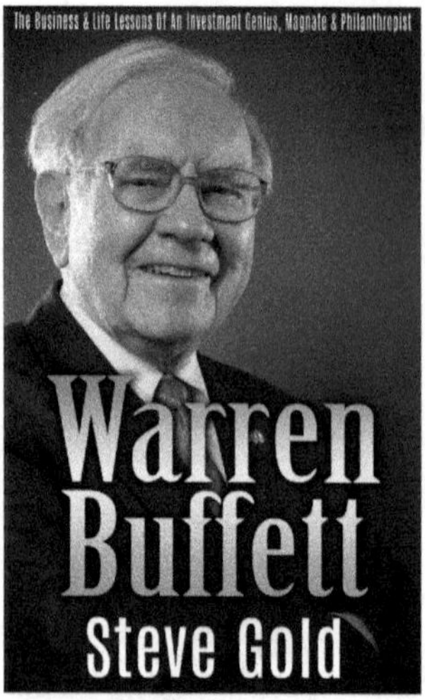

Warren Buffett - The Business And Life Lessons Of An Investment Genius, Magnate And Philanthropist

Steve Jobs - The Biography & Lessons Of The Mastermind Behind Apple

Management - Achieve Management Excellence & World Class Leadership Skills In 7 Simple Steps

Sales - Easily Sell Anything To Anyone & Achieve Sales Excellence In 7 Simple Steps

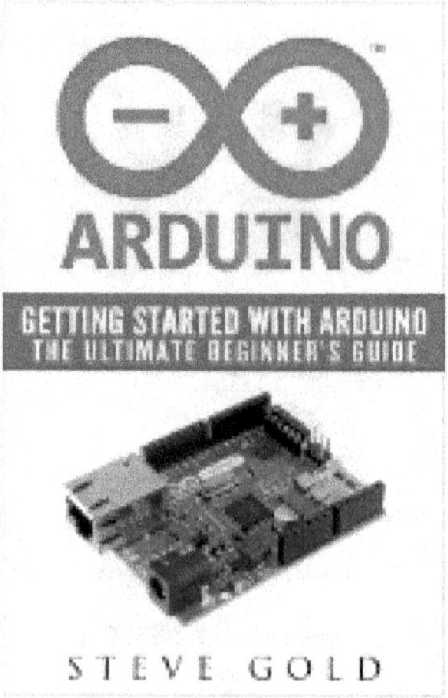
ARDUINO
GETTING STARTED WITH ARDUINO
THE ULTIMATE BEGINNER'S GUIDE
STEVE GOLD

Arduino - Getting Started With Arduino: The Ultimate Beginner's Guide

All books available as ebooks or printed books

www.ingramcontent.com/pod-product-compliance
Lightning Source LLC
Chambersburg PA
CBHW071149050326
40689CB00011B/2034
* 9 7 8 1 5 4 3 1 6 1 1 4 4 *